GRAVE QUEST
A FORGOTTEN LEGACY

By Verla Clemens

Prologue

For one hundred sixteen years a grave stood alone, unattended, on a lonely windswept hill. There is no name on the broken headstone, illegible and worn from sun and neglect. Stories have been told and retold, but none were ever certain, of the young man killed in 1886 and buried there. This is the chronicle of his legend.

Another vibrant sunset spread across the southern Arizona sky as I sat on my porch gazing out across the vast Sonoran desert. It was October of 2001, and the evening was cooling down rapidly after a dry, windy day. At the time I was living in an area not far from Willcox, Arizona, where the history of the Apaches and the Old West still lingers in the sound of the wind and shadows of the mountains. From my porch I could see Cochise's Stronghold in the western distance, where it is said he was buried some time in 1872. I'd read much of the history of the area after moving there and it never ceased to captivate my imagination.

A week or so earlier I had come across a newspaper article about a local man who had traced his family back to the Civil War and learned many surprising facts about his past. Pondering this I gazed northeast toward the Dragoon Mountains and wondered about my great-grandfather, James Quigley. I recalled the stories my parents had told me about him when I was young and was always fascinated as I imagined him living in the Old West.

The stories said he was killed in a gunfight in a place called Cow Springs, New Mexico, in June of 1886. Everyone in my family became interested in his story, but none undertook the task of trying to unravel the mystery and find his grave.

I began digging in my boxes of keepsakes and finally found the article from the Silver City newspaper my sister-in-law, Kelly, had sent me. Elated, I felt driven to begin a quest for the location of James Quigley's burial site and anything I could learn about his past. Armed with the article, maps, and anticipation of a discovery, I decided to attempt locating his grave, which had remained unknown for 116 years.

I knew it would be quite a challenge, since old birth

and death records were not always accurate and many had been destroyed by various catastrophes. New Mexico was still a territory then and any form of government was localized, often erratic and unstable at best. The Mormons were known to keep records, but that resource had limitations.

The phone rang bringing me back to reality and the present. My friend, Louise, asked me to ride into Tucson with her the next day. She was a fun, adventurous lady and we got on well. On the way to Tucson I told her about my curiosity and the history of James Quigley as I knew it. She listened intently, visibly intrigued by my story. It occurred to me that perhaps she would like to join me in my mission to find out more about James Quigley. Together, we devised a plan to take on the challenge of finding his grave. In the meantime, I continued to write down all I could recall and began making plans for our adventure.

Early in May we packed the car and headed out onto Interstate 10 east through Willcox, and across the Arizona-New Mexico state line. It was about a hundred and fifty miles to Silver City, all easy driving. The day had dawned clear and warm and the desert was in full bloom. Rather than the dull browns and yellows of winter, it had come alive with the spring rain and burst forth in a palette of color.

We reached Silver City around noon and stopped to have lunch at a small café where we talked with the owner, learning about some of the local lore and tourist sites. This was an old mining town with much fascinating history dating back beyond Cochise's time, and was also known as the home of Billy the Kid.

After lunch our first stop was the museum, a wonderful old house restored to its former state of grace, which offered a wealth of information about the area. A few files in the archive dated back to the period we sought and finally we located a card indicating James Quigley had worked at the Gold Hill mine in White Water, a small community about 15 miles south of Silver City.

That was our first find and we were both excited; hot on the trail. The next stop was the library, where we searched old microfilms and found the article about the shooting. To our surprise we also found an article his mother, Hannah Walsh, had requested the newspaper publish. Hannah wanted to give her account of the shooting of James Quigley, a sad story about the death of her only son. The original announcement that was published had made James appear as a desperado. The man who shot him, John Dodson, was depicted as a well-respected young man about town. Hannah wanted to set the record straight.

Next we went to the Mormon Church to explore their archives since they were known to keep quite accurate records of family histories. The librarian there suggested we check the 1885 Census for Grant County. Hannah Walsh was listed as head of household, a saloonkeeper, age forty seven. James was listed as a laborer, age twenty six. Also listed was James' sister, Mary (Louise), age fourteen, the father from Texas and the mother, Hannah, from Ireland. There was nothing about James' wife, Mary, and their three small boys, who lived in Gage, New Mexico, a small town about 25 miles south from Silver City.

We still had not found an obituary on James, but in

those days they generally buried the deceased shortly after death. Since the shooting had occurred on June 28th, in the heat of summer, there was little chance the body would have been moved far from where death struck.

After an exhausting day we decided to drive to Deming, the eastern part of a triangle of towns which included Silver City and Lordsburg. Cow Springs was somewhere in the area, but we had a lot of territory to consider.

That night neither Louise nor I slept well, both being keyed up and anxious to get on with our search. Next morning we awoke with a renewed sense of determination to find Cow Springs and James Quigley's grave. After breakfast, I told Louise we needed to find the oldest cemetery and mortuary in town and perhaps they could give us a clue.

The waitress at the cafe gave us directions to the oldest mortuary, and as we entered three men dressed in customary funeral black were there to greet us. With their hands clasped in front of them and in a very solemn voice one of them said, "May we help you?"

"Well, maybe," I said with a grin. At that they gave me curious looks. "I'm searching for an old grave and I thought you might be able to help me. James Quigley was my great-grandfather and we are in search of his grave. He was shot and killed back in June of 1886." The surprised expression on their faces was one I'll never forget. After explaining our quest to them, they told us their records only went back as far as 1900.

Our next stop was the Deming museum, which I entered with steeled determination. A man who had come in just behind us had overheard our inquiry about the location Gage and Cow Springs. He said he had a topographical map of the area and offered to help. He went out to his car and in a few minutes was back with his map and we located Gage.

He said there was a large sign on Interstate 10 that we couldn't miss, but there was no town anymore. Then he found Cow Springs Ranch on the map, 18 miles north of Gage, and thought it was currently owned by a private party.

Later I learned Cow Springs had been a Butterfield Stage stop and an area frequented by Indians and Mexicans. It was also known as Ojo De La Vaca (Eye of the Cow). We left Deming and drove 30 miles west to find what remained of Gage.

There was a big sign on the interstate just as the fellow with the map had said. At the gift shop there we

pulled off and went in. After
questioning the clerk about
the possibility of an old
cemetery in the area we were
told Gage was basically a
ghost town.

She said we could see
what little was left of it if we
crossed under the freeway. At
that, I felt my heart drop. I
was beginning to fear we
might never find the grave.
When we arrived at what was
left of Gage all we found was
rubble, the merest remnants of
a town.

I stood there gazing out
across that god-forsaken place
in the New Mexico desert, my
heart heavy with
disappointment, when
suddenly a small voice in my
head said, "Go on! Don't stop
now." In every direction all I
could see was mesquite and
cactus for miles beneath a
clear blue sky.

"Well, Louise," I said
turning in the wind toward my
friend, who was looking
rather depressed as well, "the

man said Cow Springs was just 18 miles north of here. Let's give it a shot."

The road was rutted and dusty and the area became more and more desolate the further we drove. As we came up to a fork in the road, I could hardly read the dusty faded sign wired to a fence post. Elated at what I found, I cried, "Yes!!" It said Cow Springs and a faded arrow pointed to the right.

We traveled on slowly trying to avoid the worst ruts for 18 miles down that road, each mile trying our patience more than the last. Finally, I told Louise, "Let's go to the top of the next hill and if we don't see anything we'll have to call this quest for the grave a wash. At least I can say we gave it our best shot."

Again the small voice in my head said, "Don't stop now!" As we topped the hill there was a cattle guard and off to the side a very faded sign that read Cow Springs Ranch. Off in the distance my eyes zoomed in on a barely visible tiny white spot.

Now, with renewed vigor, I looked at Louise and laughed. She had been ready to turn around, but now she was grinning ear to ear. I felt like the cavalry ready to charge down the hill not knowing what lay ahead. My heart was pounding as we drew closer to our destination.

After another dusty 4 miles or so we turned into the yard of a ranch house. A late model truck was sitting there and a friendly dog came out to greet us as the door of the house opened. A young man stepped out and introduced himself as Justin Turner, the ranch owner. After explaining to him who we were and the grave we sought, he took off his hat, scratched his head, and then what he told us is the reason I've written this book.

GRAVE QUEST
A Forgotten Legacy

By Verla Clemens

Chapter I

It was a gloomy afternoon at the docks in Liverpool, England, where the J.C. Cooke was moored. A scattering of well-wishers was trying to fend off the chilling September rain as Hannah and Jim Quigley boarded the ship, along with several other families. The year was 1859, and twenty-year-old Hannah was in her final term of pregnancy, due to deliver the last week of October. Her husband, Jim, was trying to comfort her, saying the captain had told him it would be a smooth trip to the new world, America. Her eyes said she was not quite convinced.

They had booked their

passage as third-class passengers and their quarters toward the aft section of the ship consisted of a small, dank and smelly room with two sagging bunks, a wobbly table, and a small stool. In one corner stood a chamber pot attached to a small table into which a basin was set, and beside it was a pail for water. Everything was more than well-worn and in need of cleaning. There were two nets stretched across the walls opposite the bunks for stowing their belongings in the cramped quarters. Hannah went about tidying up the table and sink while Jim was putting their meager belongings out of the way. There was little room to move about, so everything needed to be put up off the floor or under the lower bunk.

They had brought as much dried food as they could hoping it would be enough to last them for the journey. Hannah placed a crock of milk in the basin, added some water to keep it cool, and wondered when she would be able to get more. A short time later they sat wearily at the little table, Jim on the wooden chest that held most of their possessions, and ate some biscuits and jerky with a little of the milk. Nearly half the day was gone by the time the ship was loaded and set to sail.

"I'll go see where they've stowed the rest of our belongin's in the cargo hold," Jim told Hannah. "Why don't you take a little rest? You look a bit spent, my girl." He gave her a peck on the forehead and with his warm blue eyes and loving smile she felt a little more secure. It would be a long and arduous trip she knew, but having Jim there gave her courage she was certain to need.

Hannah spread their blankets on the bunks and lay down on the lower one to rest her back. She was awakened by shouts of, "Hoist the mast, ropes aweigh!" from the deckhands as the ship began to move away from the dock. She quickly searched for a porthole along the gangway large enough to get a look outside. Seeing the friends and families waving farewell from the dock moved her to tears. With a heavy heart she watched England disappear into the mist. The future loomed grimly before her, large and full of the unknown. Hannah was leaving everyone she had ever known, save Jim, far behind and she knew she might never see her homeland again. She was born with a courageous heart, this perky Irish colleen, but just at that moment she found herself a bit teary and weak in the knees.

Jim and Hannah had left their homeland of Ireland under the most severe conditions. The summer of 1857 brought the terrible

drought and few potatoes had
been harvested. For Ireland
this was devastating.
Starvation and conditions
brought on by lack of food
took the lives of thousands.
Hannah's father and mother
had both suffered such a fate.
Hannah, the youngest of five
children, was a winsome girl
and wise beyond her years.
She knew she couldn't stay in
the little town of Clonmell
any longer. Rather than be a
continued burden to her older
siblings she and Jim decided
it was time to give it a go on
their own.

Jim had been working as
a fisherman when he heard of
the great opportunities in the
new world called America
from seagoing men at the
wharf. With amazement in
their voices they told stories
of unbelievable prosperity;
that a person could walk along
the beach and pick up pieces
of gold or silver as big as
half-pence. Even though the
stories seemed a little far-

fetched, yet realizing a future in Ireland was bleak due to the devastation of the famine, he was filled with anxious hope for a better life in America.

Hannah was a beautiful young colleen with dark auburn hair, blue eyes, and skin like peaches and cream. In Ireland she had been working in a pub her uncle owned in Clonmell, where she waited tables and helped cook, and it was there she had met Jim. She was impressed by his strength of character and knew he would be a good provider and protector.

Jim was a handsome and friendly young man with dark curly hair and inquisitive blue eyes, an honest and caring gent. Everyone seemed to take a liking to him. He was strong and tan from working the nets on fishing boats since he was twelve years old, but had developed a kindly manner. He had been instantly overcome by Hannah's beauty and gentle nature from the moment they met. He was eight years older than Hannah and was enchanted by her determined spirit and musical laughter.

Following a whirlwind courtship, they were married in County Cork, in a small ceremony the first day of February in 1858. Jim's friend, Jack and Hannah's best friend, Mindy stood up for them, joined by a few family members and close friends. It was a bittersweet occasion, as Jim and Hannah were saying farewell after the wedding festivities, most likely to never return to Ireland again. The following morning they departed for England leaving the famine-ravaged Ireland behind. Parting with their families was not an easy thing, yet many Irish were forced to do so as a matter of survival. The fewer to feed in Ireland, the more would survive the famine.

Upon arriving in

England, Jim began driving a beer wagon for a prosperous little brewery. Hannah worked in a small pub near the home where they lived with Jim's relatives on the outskirts of Liverpool. Jim's Uncle George and Aunt Martha had moved to England four years earlier and had invited Jim and Hannah to stay with them until they were ready to depart for America.

London had become extremely crowded as people waited their turn to sail to the new world. All ships had been booked months in advance and anticipation ran high among those who were departing for America. Perhaps James and Hannah would find new hope, great fortune, even at least a better life than what existed for them in Ireland.

Chapter 2

Two weeks had passed since Jim and Hannah had said farewell to their friends and relatives at Liverpool docks. For the most part Hannah had not minded the trip so far, enjoying the fresh sea air and making new friends aboard the J.C. Cooke. That morning, though, she had not felt particularly well.

The night had been long and sleepless, as there was a storm off the bow, the wind had been howling and the sea was roiling. Several passengers had suffered seasickness throughout the long night. Finally, about noon, the sea began to grow calmer so Hannah went to their quarters to lie down for a nap. Jim had been visiting with some of the new friends they had made on board, sharing their hopes and dreams of life in America.

Suddenly Hannah awoke
with an intense pain in her
back. Clenching her fists and
moaning, she was certain she
had never felt anything like
that before. She lay back
down and waited for the pain
to subside. The sensation of
cramping spread across her
abdomen and through her
lower back. Her baby was
making himself known and
Hannah knew her time had
come.

About a half hour passed
when Hannah had another
sharp pain in her back.
Maggie was passing the
doorway when she heard
Hannah moan. Knowing the
baby wasn't supposed to be
due for another two weeks,
Maggie rapped on the door.
"That you, Hannah?" she
asked as she entered. Sizing
up the situation and seeing
the pallor on Hannah's face,
Maggie told her to lie down
while she got a cool cloth for
her forehead.

Maggie, a petite,
cheerful Swiss lady and her

husband, Hans had become acquainted with Jim and Hannah shortly after they had departed from Liverpool. They had two sons, Peter, 10, and Jake, 8 years old, who were spending much of their time with the crew learning all about seamanship. Hans and Maggie were planning to raise cattle in a place called Texas in the new world. They were told they could homestead land at no cost and start up their herd. They would be staying aboard the J.C. Cooke after it left New York and traveling on to Port of Galveston, Texas.

Hans was a big, friendly German. He loved to play his fiddle, singing and entertaining the passengers, helping to dispel the fear and apprehension they all shared. Hans and Jim had struck up a fine friendship and Maggie had taken to Hannah like a sister. They all missed their friends from their homelands and felt the effects of being displaced persons as they ventured into the unknown. Having new friends was critical to their emotional survival so they were grateful for each other's good company.

Returning with the cloth, Maggie saw the fear in young Hannah's face as another pain began. "Now you try to relax and breathe deeply with these pains, Hannah," Maggie said gently. "Don't be worried, I'll be right here with you to bring that child along. Let me go find Hans, I'll be back in a moment." Maggie found Hans and told him to go quickly and tell Jim that Hannah's labor had begun.

"Take Jim into the other room," Maggie told Hans when they came to the door. To Jim she said, "Don't worry, Jim, I've delivered babies before, a number of times, and I don't see there should be any complications here." Then she sent Hans for hot water and clean cloths and the ordeal began.

During the wee hours of the morning on the fifteenth of October in 1859, a beautiful baby boy arrived weighing about six pounds, with a healthy and very loud voice letting the world know he was there. Jim hugged Maggie so tightly that, laughing, she begged him to stop. "Jim you can go inside now and see your wife and beautiful son." Jim couldn't thank Maggie enough. "You need to thank Hannah. She did all the work," Maggie said as she left the room.

In awe he went to Hannah as she lay with James in her arms. He kissed her gently and then kissed the baby's forehead. There were tears of joy in his eyes as he sat down beside them. He was so thrilled with his new son that the next day he took the child through the entire ship for all to see and admire. The name they had chosen for the baby was James Lewis. James was for Jim's father and

Lewis for Hannah's father. It was to be an honorable and fitting name for a fine son.

Chapter 3

On the afternoon of the twenty-eighth of October in 1859, the ship moored in the New York harbor and anxious passengers disembarked. Hannah, Jim and the new baby bid a tearful farewell to Hans, Maggie, Peter, and Jake, then collected their belongings and walked off into the unfamiliar surroundings of New York and a new life.

They stared about in wonder at so many people and all the buildings being erected on every corner. It was so unlike anyplace they had ever been before. Jim placed his arm protectively about Hannah's shoulders as they headed toward the immigration center to inquire about living quarters. Hannah was filled with apprehension as they took in the sights about them on the way. Everything seemed so different from Ireland, and even England. She hoped they would be able to adjust quickly and fit in.

Jim found work as a longshoreman after spending long hours searching for a job. He worked on the docks at the harbor in New York loading and unloading cargo. He and Hannah had found a small flat on the south side of the city that was affordable and met their needs. Primarily inhabited by the Irish, the people in that area reminded Jim and Hannah of home, but it was a slovenly and perilous neighborhood.

The Irish were considered trash by the greater population of the city and suffered constant derision and harassment. Anyone with an Irish brogue would be discriminated against when it came to employment, public service, and any situation in general. Try as he would, Jim could not speak without the brogue of his homeland. It was a desperate and difficult time for the poor people from Ireland, who had already suffered terribly because of the potato famine.

The oppression wore visibly on Hannah and she constantly worried about Jim being attacked or worse. They made a few friends in the flats in their building, but rarely ventured out after dusk. The streets weren't safe for the likes of them, for the "toughs" ran the neighborhood after dark. Jim got into a couple of small scrapes, but tried to avoid trouble, as did most of the other fellows with families.

They had been in New York for two years and Hannah was anxious to escape the prejudice and despair of the city when a letter arrived from Hans and Maggie. In it Hans, once again, told them they should consider coming to Texas to homestead. Hans and Maggie were homesteading a hundred acres and said they could certainly use Jim and Hannah's help. The pay would be good and it would give Jim and Hannah an opportunity to get their own homestead someday and leave the oppression of New York behind. On the plains of Texas, and elsewhere, the Irish were treated with much less discrimination.

Optimism fluttered in Hannah's heart with Hans' encouragement. She did not want to raise her children in New York, not one bit! She and Jim had talked about going out west to settle and had read every bit of news in the papers to learn all they could.

They knew there were great dangers, but they had already faced danger, only this time they had a child to consider. Following another run-in with one of the "toughs" and harassment by the police, Jim was ready to leave New York. "It can't be much more dangerous out there than it is here for us," Jim told Hannah scowling.

In their letter Hans and Maggie offered to help them in starting up a herd of Texas longhorn cattle. This breed of steer had been bred for endurance to live in the deserts of Texas and Mexico. They would graze on most any edible vegetation and were, for the most part, quite subdued; however, they could be very unpredictable but they provided good beef. Hans did mention that there were outlaws and Indians to contend with, but that didn't seem terribly unreasonable as there was money to be made selling cattle to the cavalry.

He explained how the settlers worked together to protect their land and helped each other build homes, barns, and pens, as well as working their cattle as a cooperative. When it was time to drive

them, they would all pitch in
and drive them to the sale
pens or army posts. There was
a sense of group effort that
fended off not only enemies,
but the sense of loneliness
fostered by the expansive
plains country. It was a
convincing letter and Jim and
Hannah decided to give it a
go.

Jim, Hannah and baby
James left for Texas on the
second of October of 1861.
They boarded the train bound
for St. Louis, Missouri, early
in the sultry afternoon. The
sky was overcast as they
pulled out of the depot,
waving farewell to friends
who had come to see them off.
Once again Hannah drew on
her inborn Irish courage as
she faced the uncertainty of
relocating to a strange land.
Jim was reassuring and a
comfort to her. She
especially appreciated his
strength and patience, since
baby James was cutting teeth
and cranky most of the time

and Hannah got little rest
from the energetic little tyke.

It was autumn and the
colors were spectacular
throughout the countryside.
Hannah would sit at the train
window with little James on
her lap pointing at all the
colorful trees and harvested
fields as they went by. She
had often missed the beauty of
her home in Ireland while
living in New York, but
looking out upon this vibrant
landscape she felt hope surge
in her breast.

At least, now, they
would have an opportunity for
a more prosperous future with
their own ranch and cattle.
She had read about Texas in
the newspapers and it seemed,
since the Civil War, that it
held great promise. There
were hair-raising accounts of
Indian encounters, and
without a doubt, they gave
Hannah much to be concerned
about. But the thought of
having their own place, open

and free, was stronger than the fear, and so she resolved to think only of the good possibilities and put the fearful ones aside.

From St. Louis they would travel by a local stage line to Tipton, Missouri. They had booked passage from Tipton on the new Butterfield Express stage line, which would take them on to Austin Texas. Jim had not been feeling well since shortly after leaving New York; he'd been feverish and irritable for several days.

By the time they arrived in Tipton he was very ill and they had to find a doctor quickly. The doctor advised them to stay over for a few days to see if Jim would improve. The news was not good and their stay was more than a week. Jim had symptoms of cholera and it was feared he might not recover. The doctor thought Jim might have contracted the disease in his last days working on the docks. He was put in isolation where his condition rapidly worsened. The morning of October twelfth Jim passed on.

Hannah was heartbroken, her dreams shattered by Jim's death. Her courage seemed to ebb away, but when she looked at little James she knew she had to go on. Now it was up to her to raise their son as best she could and provide for them both somehow.

Hannah now faced the greatest challenge in her life. There she was in a country she knew little about, not even sure where she was going, some little town near Austin, much less how she would get on. Doctor White and his wife, June had put Hannah and little James up in their home while Jim was in isolation. June had seen the fear in Hannah eyes. Putting her arms around Hannah to comfort her, she had told her "Anything you need or want just tell us. We will be here to help you and your son until you are ready to move on." June's words were the comfort that Hannah needed to bear her overwhelming sorrow. After Jim's death, Dr. White and June helped with burial arrangements and made sure Hannah was ready to travel before her departure to Texas.

Hannah's only consolation was the fact that Hans and Maggie were dear friends and would be ready and willing to help her. It was that prospect that kept her from simply giving up altogether. She summoned all the courage she could muster and after burying her husband she became determined to carry on. Hannah and James resumed their journey to Austin in sorrow and anxiety.

Hans and Maggie were at the stage station to meet Hannah and James. "Look at this child!" Maggie lifted James up to give him a hug while Hannah told them all that had happened. Hans, with tears in his eyes, put his big arms around Hannah and told her not to worry. He and Maggie would see to it that she had a home and all she needed to raise baby James.

"Don't you worry about a thing," Maggie told her warmly. "You're part of our family now." She put James down on the ground, took his little hand and put her other arm around Hannah's shoulders giving her a warm smile. "The wagon's over around the corner. Let's get on home."

They went quietly then to Hans and Maggie's place. It was a simple one-story house with an attached shed in which all the cooking was done. Maggie had a fine garden at the south side of the house and Hans had built a large barn beyond the windmill for storing fodder, with a handy milking area complete with stanchions and a natural creek running through to keep the cans cold after milking.

He was selling milk and cream in town with regularity and folks knew his place was clean as a whistle, which meant less chance of disease. He had three hundred head of beef cattle, Texas longhorns, out on the range and was building that to a larger herd before selling. He anticipated being able to cut out a third of the steers for sale in the spring after the calving season.

Seeing how well Hans and Maggie had done in the brief time they'd been in Texas gave Hannah hope, yet she also felt deep sorrow that Jim couldn't be there to homestead for them. This was what they had dreamed about, hoped for, and now Jim was gone. Hannah felt the

overwhelming loss and sorrow
that first night at the ranch as
she put James to bed.
Exhausted and sad she
climbed into bed and
whispered, "Wherever you are,
Jim darlin', I'm hopin' you'll
stay close by a while till I get
my feet on the ground here.
I'll need you to keep an eye
on your son as well, you
know," she smiled into the
dimly lit room. The oil lamp
on the table by her bed
flickered ever so slightly and
Hannah took it as a sign. She
sighed, blew a kiss across the
room, and put out the lamp.
Sleep came to Hannah swiftly
and peacefully. She prayed
they would be fine here in
Texas.

Chapter 4

Hannah and James had been living with Hans and Maggie for nearly six years and had truly felt like part of their family. They had all worked very hard to make the ranch successful and had done quite well. Not only had it provided a home for Hannah and James, it had also served as excellent training for the young lad for a life of self-sufficiency in the West. He, Jake, and Peter had become as brothers and James looked up to them with deep respect.

The boys had all grown like weeds and were enjoying their lives on the ranch. Tanned and healthy they claimed they could all ride like Comanche, whom they had seen only a few times. Hans relished their enthusiasm and liveliness, though sometimes he winced at their bravado.

His pride in his young

partners was evident. Theirs was a respected outfit among all the local ranchers and their ranch had prospered well. Jake and Peter, being in their teens, had learned much from Hans about ranching and working the cattle and thus, had become wise in the ways of this new frontier. It was fortunate that the boys were strong and capable.

One morning in February Hans heard a considerable noise in the bull pen and went out to investigate. One side of the rails had been torn down and two of his prize bulls had managed to get into the same pen and were fighting, trying to kill each other. When Hans tried to separate them he was gored by one of the bulls. James heard the ruckus and went out to see what was going on. Seeing Hans lying in a pool of blood, James ran as fast as he could yelling for Peter. He was about out of breath when he found him in the barn. "Come quickly!

Your father has been hurt in the bull pens," James said, trying to catch his breath.

By the time they got to the pens Hans had crawled under the fence and was lying there bleeding from a large wound in his gut. Maggie and Hannah had also heard the commotion and when they got to Hans he had passed out from losing so much blood. They got him into the house and sent Peter for the doctor, but he never regained consciousness and died of his wound that night.

It was a terrible loss for the whole family, as Hans had been the bulwark for the entire enterprise. Everyone looked to him for advice and training. He was a well-respected man and had contributed much to helping build a foundation of friendship and mutual help within the community. Following a large funeral, he was laid to rest on the hill overlooking the ranch. Peter, Jake and James put a white picket fence around the grave. Virtually everyone in the community had come to Han's funeral. He had touched many folks' hearts.

Maggie, Jake, Peter, Hannah, and James were left to manage the ranch. It was now more than a thousand acres in size with a herd of five hundred fifty head of longhorns. Now Maggie turned to Hannah for her support and comfort. For days Maggie cried and Hannah would hold her tight and tell her, "Maggie, I know how you feel and I'm here for you just as you were for me when I lost Jim. Only time will heal your hurt but together we can make it. We're strong women who have endured the worst."

Hans had sold the dairy herd the year before to some new settlers and invested the money in more longhorns. Now theirs was a heavy responsibility, but Han's boys insisted they could handle it and reassured their mother they would be fine and the ranch would continue to prosper. Through the following months the boys took over all the outdoor chores, keeping the ranch on an even keel and proving their capabilities.

In the spring they all agreed they would need to hire help for the coming calving season, which would be starting in about two weeks. Hannah was busy fixing dinner when she heard a knock at the door. She opened it and stood there, suddenly unable to speak. There stood a tall, handsome cowboy asking about a job as cowhand. Hannah swallowed and forced words from her lips while his eyes were riveted on hers. "Yes...well, you might go on out to the barn and speak with Peter or Jake," she said softly, trying to catch her breath.

With a warm smile and twinkle in his eyes the cowboy spoke as he turned to go. "Thank ya, ma'am. I'll do that." Then he was gone. Hannah stood for a long time gazing into the darkness of late evening, her breath coming unevenly. She realized he was gone and went mechanically back to preparing dinner, and noticed her hands quivering slightly.

While she worked at the stove she pictured him again, tall, dark hair, with dark flashing eyes, perhaps a mix of white and Indian or Spanish blood, ever so handsome. She hadn't seen a man that handsome in a very long time. Suddenly she felt the warmth of a blush and hoped it hadn't shown when he was standing there at the door!

It was suppertime when James and the stranger finally came through the door. "Mother, this is Matt Isatine, our new cowhand," James told her. Once again Hannah felt the blush and prayed fervently that no one noticed as she set another place at the table.

After dinner while she cleared the table Matt stood up and started toward the door. "I'm mighty glad to be hired on a place with such a fine cook," he told her with a wink. Some of these outfits feed their hands like they do their cattle!"

"I think I can do better than that," she laughed and blushed as he turned and went out the door to the bunkhouse. From that evening on Hannah looked forward to Matt coming in for his meals, and she made sure she always looked her best.

A month later things had started to slow down after the the major amount of calving had taken place. The boys and Maggie had decided to keep on the men they had hired as they would be needed as the ranch continued to grow. The ranch hands would play poker on the porch of the bunkhouse until late in the evenings and Hannah always listened for Matt's voice. One evening after dinner he stayed around and started a conversation with her. "I understand you lost your husband before he ever got to see Texas," he said to her quietly. When she nodded he went on. "That's a shame. A pretty lady like yourself should have a man to take care of you and start a ranch of your own."

Everyone else had left the house so Hannah offered Matt a cup of coffee and they sat down to talk. He was an interesting man with an easy laugh and casual manner that made Hannah feel like a young woman again. When he rose to leave he paused by the door, then turned and swept Hannah into his arms and pressed his warm lips to hers. At first she resisted, but the kiss was warm and sweet and she felt herself relenting. She was certain she had never been kissed like that before and responded to his embrace.

They both felt the passion pulsing through them, pressing their bodies into each other. It had been so long for Hannah since a man had held her like that and she felt her resistance ebbing away. Then Matt picked her up and carried her into the bedroom and laid her gently on the bed, all the while kissing her neck, her face, and her lips in heated passion.

His touch was commanding yet gentle and Hannah succumbed to his charms. Matt was so exciting she was compelled to respond to his every move, giving back passion for passion until they both lay breathless, locked in their embrace. Hannah wished the ecstasy could last forever.

It was near midnight

when Matt woke Hannah. "I'd better be getting over to the bunkhouse," he told her. "I don't want to start up gossip," he said winking. When he leaned over to kiss her the feeling came over both of them again and the love-making was even better than the first time.

Matt got dressed then, leaving a sweet kiss on Hannah's lips as he slipped out the door and into the night. Hannah lay there for a long time reliving the wonderful moments of their lovemaking before finally falling asleep.

She was startled awake the next morning with a knock on her door. "Mother, are you all right?" James called. She jumped out of bed and opened the door, twisting her hair into a bun and smoothing her dress. "Mother its seven o'clock. I was afraid you might be sick since breakfast isn't ready yet."

"Ohh, I'm so sorry. Guess I was more tired last night than I thought," she said hastily, as she scurried about to get the bacon started. She hoped she didn't look too embarrassed. She still had a warm feeling from the night of love and nothing was going to upset her this morning, not even a bunch of hungry cowhands.

Matt came in about twenty minutes later, and when Hannah saw him the butterflies started to flutter in her stomach as he gave her a grin. She started to blush all over again and quickly went into the pantry to conceal her flushed face. She surely didn't want the other boys to see her turning red.

Maggie came into the kitchen a little later that morning, and Hannah came up from the cellar and found her leaning against the wall looking very pale. Maggie admitted she had not been feeling well that week. After Hannah pressed her about her ailment Maggie confessed she had been passing blood in her urine and her back had been hurting for a couple of weeks.

"You're going into town and see Dr. Brooke," Hannah said exasperated. Hannah had Peter bring up the buckboard and together they drove Maggie into town that morning.

Dr. Brooke came out of the examining room and told Hannah, "I'm afraid this looks very serious. I would like to have Maggie go to the hospital for some tests. Hannah arranged to take Maggie to Austin and Peter insisted on accompanying them, leaving Jake and James, with Matt's help, to take care of the ranch. It was a hard trip for Maggie and Hannah felt completely helpless trying to ease her pain and help her.

The hospital staff was

gracious and did their best to make Maggie comfortable when she arrived, giving her some medication quickly to ease the agony from the trip. The hospital was a very recent and badly needed addition to Austin. Hannah was grateful it took no more than two hours in the buckboard to get there. She feared Maggie wouldn't have survived a longer trip. She and Peter found a rooming house just down the street so they could be nearby.

Their stay lasted a week and the result of the tests was that Maggie had cancer of the bladder. She was growing weaker by the day and the doctors said she only had a couple of months to live.

Hannah was utterly devastated. Maggie had been her best friend and the prospect of losing her was almost more than she could bear. She and Peter drew from each other the courage and strength it took to face the grim days ahead. They took Maggie back to the ranch and tried to make her as comfortable as possible. Everyone from the little community stopped by to pay Maggie a visit and tried to cheer her some. Hannah and the boys did all they could to make her last days easier, and she left Maggie's side only long enough to do the most necessary chores. Matt would stop in every morning to see how he could help Hannah before going out on the range. Occasionally he would bring in some bluebonnet flowers from Maggie's garden to cheer Maggie, knowing she loved flowers so.

In the evenings he would stay and help clear the dishes and wait while Hannah got Maggie comfortable for the night. Some evenings they would sit on the porch for a few blissful minutes before retiring, and he would console Hannah and hold her for a little while. It helped her immensely through the terrible ordeal of seeing her dearest friend slip away.

Maggie's condition worsened with each passing day, but she somehow managed to keep a cheerful countenance right up to the end, in spite of the terrible pain she endured. She would smile and say, "I know Hans is waiting for me to join him." The day she closed her eyes in death was incredibly sad for Hannah and the boys. Peter and Jake made the funeral arrangements and Maggie was laid to rest beside Hans on the hill. Guests came from everywhere bearing food. Hans and Maggie had endeared themselves to everyone in the community and were not to be soon forgotten.

Hannah felt like she had been set adrift in the sea of life. She looked to James and

Maggie's sons for strength and courage in that week of Maggie's passing. Matt had gone to Abilene to bring some new bulls to the ranch from a sale so he wasn't there for moral support, although he was surely on Hannah's mind.

Matt and Hannah were together regularly when he was home, and it became obvious they were falling in love. Matt finally asked Hannah to marry him a month after Maggie's death. Hannah was ready to get married again; after all, it had been a long time since Jim had died and she enjoyed having a man in her life again.

James took the news well, as did the other boys, and they welcomed Matt by making him their ranch foreman. The wedding was a small and personal affair with just family and close friends. When autumn came the ranch was bustling with activity as crops were put up for the winter. Wood was stacked against the chill of the coming evenings and Hannah dried and canned food for the family.

Most evenings there was little talk at the supper table, as everyone was near spent and thinking only of the badly needed rest they would get when winter finally arrived. They had done very well that year, considering the sadness they'd had to endure with the loss of both Hans and Maggie. The herd had grown and pastures were green and healthy even after the first frost. There was plenty of grain and fodder in the barns and food in the pantry, and the whole community had celebrated the plentiful harvest with a festival the end of October.

The little community had grown considerably over the past two years and was finally given the name of Smoot for the first family to settle there. They had a fine school, a reputable town council, a decent hotel, and the cafe was excellent, with its own bakery. The folks in town were good, law-abiding people and wouldn't stand for outlaws coming in and causing trouble.

There was one incident and one only, and the people came together like a pack of angry dogs and ran three hustlers out of town on a cold February day, and there hadn't been any trouble since. Even the Comanches left the folks of Smoot alone when they were out on their raiding sprees. They generally raided a little further north or west, so other ranchers in the area weren't bothered either.

Now and then a steer would be missing, but the ranchers considered it a small price to pay for the safety and welfare of the entire community. Since the ranching had made hunting more difficult for the Comanche, the ranchers understood and agreed that as long as it was only occasionally they took a steer there would be no repercussion. It was a mutual unspoken agreement between natives and ranchers and it served them both well.

It wasn't long after the harvest festival that Matt seemed to change. He became edgy and surly with the cowhands and argued frequently with Peter, Jake and James. He would talk even less with Hannah, and when they went to bed he just said, "Goodnight," and went to sleep. He made more frequent trips away from the ranch and each time, when he came back, it seemed he was more on edge and snapped at everyone. He would say strange things and talked about how someday he would have plenty of money. When Hannah would confront him about it he would turn away from her and get on his horse and ride away, sometimes staying away for a week or more.

Matt barked at her if she asked him what was wrong, and kept his distance from everyone as much as possible. Hannah wasn't feeling particularly well either, and she would often cry her heart out. She didn't understand why Matt was treating her the way he was. She had always been a strong-willed lady and rarely let things like this upset her. After being prodded by her son, she agreed to go into town and see Dr. Brooke. James accompanied her in the buckboard, seeing to her safety.

"Hannah you are going to be a mother," the good doctor told her. Hannah was elated at the prospect of having a baby. She realized this would be the first baby ever at the ranch. She also remembered how Matt had been behaving and wondered how he would take the news. She could hardly keep herself still at the supper table that night as she waited anxiously to tell Matt when they were alone.

After supper when she told him, Matt didn't take the news well at all. With a dark look in his eyes she had never seen before he said, "I never wanted to have children, Hannah!" James overheard their conversation as he was approaching the back door. He turned on his heel and went quickly to the barn where he threw hay until his anger abated.

Hannah felt herself wilting before this stranger, the man she had married. He was so different now and he didn't even want his own child. Her heart felt heavy as iron as she went about her evening chores. She swore to herself she wouldn't let James know how Matt had reacted. Maybe Matt would come around in time and be happy about the baby, she thought. She was facing another difficult challenge, but this time, alone. She saw very little of Matt after that. He was either in town drinking and playing cards or away on business.

He often went to beef sales to find out about the market and to look for good bulls to improve the breeding, at least that's what he told Hannah. His time away became more frequent and lengthy as her due date drew nearer.

James distanced himself from Matt and spoke only when spoken to. When Peter and Jake questioned his sudden alienation from Matt, he just shrugged his young shoulders and shook his head. They, too, had misgivings about Matt's behavior and absences.

James stayed closer to his mother in the evenings when Matt wasn't around, which was becoming a common occurrence. James was a great comfort to Hannah, and she could only hope that the arrival of the baby would somehow change things with Matt, for him and herself.

On the fifteenth of April in 1871, Hannah gave birth to a beautiful baby girl she named Mary Louise. Even Dr. Brooke told Hannah, "She is such a beautiful baby girl." With a full head of dark curly hair and dark brown eyes, Mary Louise looked just like her father. Hannah couldn't get over the tiny perfect face and slender little fingers on her dainty hands. The boys would be so proud to have such a pretty little girl in the family.

Shortly after Mary Louise had arrived James cautioned Hannah about Matt saying he had become a different person and was no

longer trusted by himself,
Peter or Jake. He had pretty
much fallen from grace with
everyone who knew him, for
they all respected Hannah and
knew all she had been
through.

Hannah was mystified
and terribly sad about Mart's
changed personality. She
could find no good reason for
his behavior as she searched
her soul again and again for
the cause. Many nights she
wept until she fell asleep,
wondering and praying about
Matt. He didn't come home for
days at a time and refused to
look at his new daughter when
he was home. Early in June
Hannah watched Matt saddle
up and leave the ranch as a
rainstorm moved in. A heavy
feeling of fear and sorrow
filled her heart and the dark
clouds seemed an omen.

A month went by and
Matt had not returned, nor had
he been seen in Smoot or
anywhere in the area. Hannah
went into town to see the
Sheriff and report him as

missing. He hadn't been gone quite so long before and she was certain something dreadful had happened to him.

One morning in July the sheriff stopped by bringing sad news. He told Hannah that Matt had been shot in a bank hold-up in San Antonio and had died on the street in front of the bank. Hannah and the boys were stunned at the news. James stayed close to his mother consoling her and helping her cope with the shocking tragedy. With Hannah's consent, he sent money to the sheriff in San Antonio to have Matt buried there. The boys were adamant. They never wanted him back on the ranch again, ever.

Once again Hannah found herself summoning her courage to go on, only this time it was in sorrow mixed with considerable anger. She took consolation in Mary Louise and vowed to give her the best home possible.

James, Peter and Jake were all
very taken with the baby girl
and spent much of their free
time helping to care for her.
They were determined to fill
the vacancy Matt's death had
left for Hannah and did all
they could to help her forget.
For the most part Mary Louise
had all three boys wrapped
around her tiny fingers.

Chapter 5

It took quite some time for Hannah to get past the anger of Matt's abandonment and death. James was a tremendous comfort to her and helped her realize that the real blessing was having Mary Louise. She was a joy to everyone on the ranch and they all claimed some sort of kinship with her. Her bright smile and mischievous eyes won every heart that came in contact with her.

When she was old enough to sit up in the saddle she insisted on riding with James, Peter or Jake every chance she got. She was quick and alert and kept the boys constantly amused with her antics. They taught her to ride and listened to her patiently when she told them stories and wanted to sing for them. They put up a swing in one of the apple trees where she would spend hours singing

and swinging in her
daydreams.

One evening after
supper, she overheard Peter
and Jake say they were going
over to the Parkins' place to
see about some fence posts,
but they were really both
sweet on the two Parkins girls
who were about their same
ages. Mary Louise sneaked out
of the house without
detection, taking their good
boots with her, and hid them
in the chicken coop. When the
boys went to get ready to
leave they couldn't find their
boots, much to their dismay.

Mary Louise was sitting
beside James as he read to
her, watching them out of the
corner of her mischievous
little eyes. Hannah happened
to glance her way and seeing
the sly look, gave Mary
Louise a raised eyebrow that
said, "You little dickens, I
know who took those boots!"
But Hannah never uttered a
word.

The boys searched the house from floor to rafters, and were totally exasperated when Mary Louise finally gave in to the giggles. The cat was out of the bag then, and both Peter and Jake came after her. She skittered around through the kitchen, but Jake headed her off at the back door and scooped her up into his arms. Then tickling her until she begged for mercy, she told them to go to the chicken coop.

In their stocking feet they marched to the chicken coop to retrieve their boots, then with a determined look of retaliation headed straight back into the house. Mary Louise was frantically searching for a good hiding place and when they came in she tip-toed out of the pantry and slipped out the back door. They couldn't find her anywhere.

They were completely mystified. Finally Jake just

hollered, "Wherever you are Mary Louise, you had better be very careful from now on. You never know what's going to happen when you least expect it!" They left the house laughing and James and Hannah just waited for Mary Louise to come out of hiding.

After the boys were out of sight, Mary Louise lifted the washtub beside the back stoop and crawled out giggling. When she danced back into the kitchen Hannah and James laughed and told her she was quite the prankster. "But you'd best be watchful, Mary Louise," James warned her. "You know they'll think of a way to get even one day."

"No, they won't," she smiled as she snuggled into the chair beside him. "They love me too much!" The comment brought a chuckle from James as he shook his head at her knowing she spoke pure truth.

Mary Louise pretty much kept things interesting around the ranch. She had a way of being right in the middle of most things going on, even when she had no business being there. The boys would get put out with her from time to time, but she always won their forgiveness and affection. She was a very pretty little girl with a flair for the dramatic. Everything seemed to be a production with her and she kept everyone amused with her impishness.

To Hannah's satisfaction, James had grown into a fine young man, well-liked and respected. He had worked hard on the ranch helping Peter and Jake build up the herd of longhorns to twelve-hundred head, but he was getting restless and often spoke of wanting to try something else. He told Hannah he would like to try his hand at mining for a change. He was planning on taking his share of the herd to the sale in Abilene in the spring after the calving, then take a look at the New Mexico Territory. Some areas were reporting good finds of silver ore and the stories intrigued him.

James had run into some trouble a year earlier when two men tried to break into his mother's quarters at the ranch. It was about one thirty in the morning and everyone was sound asleep. When he heard glass break and Hannah scream, James grabbed his gun and ran down the hall to see what had happened.

A man was holding Hannah by the throat and demanding all their money. He told James to drop his gun and began dragging Hannah across the dining room. James was standing next to the sideboard and knew his mother always kept a small gun in one of the drawers.

He carefully edged backward toward the sideboard telling the man to let Hannah go and he would get the money. While he was speaking, James reached into the drawer and pulled out the gun. Just as the man let Hannah go, James fired and hit the man in the chest.

A moment later a scream came from Mary Louise's room. James and Hannah ran to see what had happened, and when they threw open the door they saw a man trying to tear Mary Louise's nightgown off. James grabbed him and threw him across the room. The stranger pulled a dirk out of his boot and made a lunge at him. James still had Hannah's gun and he fired, killing the man in an instant. Later they learned the two strangers were brothers and were wanted by the law. They had robbed and killed some folks up north and had a bounty on their heads of $2,500 each.

At the hearing it was proven beyond any doubt that James acted in self-defense in the killing of the two brothers. When things settled down again James told his mother about plans he had devised. He was ready to go to New Mexico and get into mining.

Hannah wasn't surprised to hear her son talking about leaving Texas. He had always had a wandering eye and a curiosity for what was over the next rise. He had worked hard on the ranch and was anxious to try something new and see new country. His spirit was contagious to Hannah and she began to feel she, too, was ready for new surroundings.

They had both worked hard and had saved their money so they would be able to relocate without the hardships they suffered when first coming to Texas. Hannah remembered the stories Jim had told her when they were coming to America about how everyone could get rich from gold and silver. Well, it hadn't been so easy as they had hoped back then, but now she and James were pretty well set.

Hannah and James had been on the ranch for sixteen years helping Peter and Jake maintain and prosper in the cattle industry. Peter, being the oldest, was in charge of all the ranch operations, and they had agreed that if the time ever came for Hannah and James to go, they would settle up with them in equal shares. With the money from the bounty and their part of the ranch and cattle Hannah, James, and Mary Louise made plans to venture further west to the New Mexico territory.

Chapter 6

It was the middle of May in 1879, when they bid Peter and Jake somber farewells and boarded the stage to El Paso, Texas. From there it would take them to Cow Springs, New Mexico, then they would go on to their intended destination of Silver City. Butterfield warned the passengers on the outset of a trip. The poster read:

YOU WILL BE TRAVELING THROUGH INDIAN COUNTRY AND THE SAFETY OF YOUR PERSON CANNOT BE VOUCHSAFED BY ANYONE BUT GOD.

The day was beginning to get warm and thunderheads were building over the

Sacramento Mountains with a promise of rain. The stage was full and James had to send some of their belongings on a later stage to allow room for the other passengers' bags. In the coach there was a newspaper man, who only went as far as Deming, a lady named Nettie, a lady perhaps just a little older than Hannah, and her niece, Mary, an attractive young lady.

Mary Louise deduced right away that it was going to be crowded in the coach, so she told James she guessed she would just have to sit on his lap the entire way to El Paso. When he winced at her, she took the opportunity to turn to the driver Gus and with a most charming smile said, "Of course, I'd be obliged to ride up top with Gus and Rex if it's okay with them." Hannah just looked at the sky while James mumbled something about not being a bit surprised at her suggestion. There was some hesitation as to her safety, but eight-year-old Mary Louise wouldn't take no for an answer, so up she went, with the understanding that it would only be until the next stage stop, three hours away. James wasn't terribly upset about Mary Louise's decision.

Hannah had packed some dried meat, fruit and biscuits she made for the trip. She had heard the food was not very good at the stage stops; that some of the food was wormy and the jerky could be bacon, venison, antelope, or mule flesh, the latter being very tough from being cooked over buffalo or cowchip fires.

For the next five days they would have a bone-jarring ride over some of the most rugged and beautiful country across the Pecos River. They were informed by the driver that they would be

going though an lay of sand
four miles in length on the
west side of the Guadalupe
Pass and they would have to
walk the four miles through
the soft sand to relieve the
horses.

Once they reached Live
Oak Creek at Fort Lancaster
Texas, they would pick up a
cavalry detachment escort
until they were safely out of
Indian Territory. It was a safe
trip, quite rough at times but
the company was pleasant.
When they had to disembark
and walk it wasn't not all that
bad it gave everyone a chance
to stretch their legs.

They had seen the
Indians far off on the bluffs,
but they never showed any
aggressions and kept their
distance. James had his pistol
under his coat as did the other
gentleman riding with them,
and they would have used
them if they were faced with a
dangerous situation.

For the most part, the

ride was not terribly unpleasant and the weather had not been unbearable. They enjoyed the gorgeous clouds tinged by the setting sun, and watched as they turned from a golden color to a deep red above the jagged peaks.

They made about five to twelve miles an hour for the five days and nights they crossed vast treeless plains, jagged mountain passes, and rivers with quicksand. The coach stopped only to change horses or hitch up raw-bone mules, and let everyone tend to their personal needs. All the drivers were courteous, civil and experienced men making the trip safe and less threatening.

James had taken the seat directly across from Nettie's niece, Mary, and she didn't seem the least bit disappointed. She was an attractive young lady just turned twenty and James couldn't keep his eyes off her. With dark hair, soft hazel-green eyes, and full expressive lips she was easily the finest woman he had ever met.

After introductions and some polite conversation, James learned that her mother was Cree Indian, and her father was from Paris, France. They had settled in the northern part of Arkansas, where both of her parents had died of the cholera plague.

"How long have you lived with your Aunt Nettie?" James inquired."

"Since I was ten years old," she told him. "She's been like a mother to me. She gave birth to a baby boy who lived only two days, and after that she was never able to conceive again."

"Is her husband still living?" James asked."

"No," Mary said tilting her head as she looked out the window of the stage. "Jeff was a horse buyer for the government. A couple of years ago, when they were bringing a herd up from Texas, a bad storm came up. He had just gotten back to camp when a bolt of lightening hit close by, and the thunder was deafening. The horses stampeded, running straight towards camp. There was no time for Jeff to get out of the way and he was trampled to death."

"That's a shame," James said nodding his head respectfully towards Nettie.

Nettie smiled at James and said, "He looked a lot like you, as a matter of fact. He was a good man. I still miss him terribly."

"I'm sorry, Ma'am," James replied, turning his hat in his hand. "And I thank ya for the compliment. That was a tough business he was in. Working with mustangs there is always some dangers."

James and Mary carried on their own conversation in softer tones while Mary Louise, having come inside the coach, slept on Hannah's lap. Hannah and Nettie visited and became acquainted as the trip wore on.

It turned out Nettie had a job in Silver City as a seamstress, working at the cavalry camp. She was a pleasant lady a few years older than Hannah and it was obvious she was quite taken with Mary Louise. Hannah and Nettie began what would become a wonderful and valued friendship.

Nettie inquired as to James' and Hannah's plans when they arrived in Silver City. James told her he had heard of men making their fortunes in mining, so he had decided to give it a try. Hannah told Nettie she was planning on opening a cafe and saloon. What with all the men coming into the territory looking for gold and silver it should be a good place to go into that kind of business.

"I've worked in pubs

in Ireland and England and
in a cafe in New York. And
then of course, I cooked
for everyone at the ranch
in Texas for fifteen years.
I think I've had plenty of
experience," she laughed.
"I thought I would at least
try having my own
business. After all, this is
the New Territory, and
there should be a lot of
opportunity out here for
both men and women."

Hannah had saved most
of her money while working
for the cattle ranch and she
knew just what she wanted her
saloon and cafe to look like.
She hoped to find a building
for sale that would fit her
needs, but was aware she may
need to consider having one
built. James planned to help
her get set up and running as
much as he could while
working in the Gold Hill
mine, where he was told he
would have no problem being
hired on.

Upon arriving at Cow Springs New Mexico early in the morning, Hannah, James, Mary Louise, Mary and Nettie were completely exhausted. The five days had taken its toll on the passengers and they were hungry, dirty, and most of all in need of a bed for a full night's sleep. A deployment of eight Buffalo soldiers from Fort Bayard had been sent to escort the new arrivals to Silver City to protect them from Apache raiders. The fifteen miles in a wagon was as bone-jarring for them as the stage coach ride had been. In spite of their fatigue, their hopes were riding high as the end of the trip neared.

When they finally arrived in Silver City they were all tired, sore, and glad to get off the wagon. It was a dusty, windy, and very uncomfortable ride, but there had been no incidents so they were grateful for that. They stayed at the hotel until they found places to live.

A week after their arrival James located a house just east of town about a half mile that was for sale. Meanwhile, Nettie and Mary found a small house in town. It was an exciting time in their lives. Hannah was able to procure a suitable building across from the livery for her saloon and cafe. She, James, and even Mary Louise, worked hard to clean and get it ready to open. It was named **The Silver City Cafe & Saloon**.

James continued to court Mary, the love of his life, and it was quite clear there would be wedding plans in the near future. He worked hard at the mine and made new friends quickly. One of the fellows he worked with, Sam Allsworth, was doing some prospecting on his own when he could get away. After talking privately to James about it, they planned to do some work together to stake a claim of their own in the Mogollon Mountains to the east of Silver City.

Mary Louise was becoming a beautiful young girl and Hannah was pleased that there was a good school in Silver City. She encouraged Mary Louise at every turn, to study hard and do well at her lessons so she would have a good education, something Hannah never had. Mary Louise was very bright and well liked, especially by the boys. She was looking more like her father, Matt, and Hannah worried occasionally, hoping she wouldn't turn out like him. At times Mary Louise would show a side of her that Hannah could see one day could get her into trouble. She was very determined, at times downright stubborn and bold, but she was a loving daughter and adored her brother, James.

On the second day of July, Hannah had the grand opening of her saloon and cafe. Folks came from miles around to have dinner and drinks and share in the fun. Hannah had gone all out to make the cafe elegant with tablecloths from New York and curtains all the way from Paris, France.

She had hired some fellas from over by Las Cruces to play music throughout the evening, and Mary Louise couldn't get enough of the singing and dancing. She was so intrigued by the piano that she determined she wanted to learn to play it herself. The experience was to have a powerful impact on the young girl's future. She began to dream of singing and playing, and did so every chance she got. Hannah had hired a man to run the saloon, by the name of Harlow Walsh, a fine, good looking gentleman in his forties, who had moved to Silver City from Boston a year or so earlier.

He had been an accountant for a law firm in

Boston, but yearned for space and adventure. He was well built and solid, so there was no hesitation in him when called on to take care of any trouble caused by anyone who got out of line in the saloon. Harlow had a casual, friendly way with the patrons, and took no guff off trail hands passing through.

The only women at the saloon were there to wait tables for meals, and occasionally they would have a singer come in. Both the saloon and cafe were to be reputable establishments by Hannah's decree.

Business was brisk and Hannah and Harlow worked well together. They seemed to have a certain rhythm in their business association. In time, it became so synchronized that before they realized it they were falling in love. They worked hard and laughed just as hard, as they enjoyed working together.

The holidays were celebrated in the finest style Hannah could conjure up. There were decorations everywhere and she had everything from tamales to corned beef and cabbage on the menu, including a few recipes Harlow had given her from the Boston area.

Mary Louise had even learned some tunes on the piano so she could help entertain. She showed not only a fine talent for the piano, but had a clear, resonant voice, and everyone enjoyed hearing her sing.

New Year's Eve, after everyone had finally gone home, Hannah and Harlow sat sipping coffee in the cafe, talking and laughing about the evening's events. "Harlow, I want to talk business here for a moment if you don't mind," she told him smiling slyly.

Tired as he was, Harlow nodded and yawned. "Just please be brief or I'll likely be asleep before you finish."

"I want you to be my partner in the business, Harlow," she said as she placed her hand on his. "I couldn't have done all this without you, and you deserve to be rewarded for all your effort and support."

"That's a very generous offer, Hannah," he replied, squeezing her hand. "I do most gratefully accept. Matter of fact, I've got an offer for you too," he whispered leaning close to her ear.

His voice tickled her ear and sent chills up her spine as she inquired about his offer. "I'd like to make you my partner, Hannah, for life. Will you marry me?"

Hannah just blinked and nodded her answer. When she recovered her voice, she squeezed his hand and kissed his cheek as she softly whispered "Yes, Harlow. Oh my yes! That is a wonderful idea! Partners till the end."

Little tears formed at the corner of her eyes and he held her close as they savored the moment that would begin the rest of their lives. It was the perfect arrangement for them both, as they were ready and time wasn't going to wait. It had been a long time since Matt was killed, and Jim was a faint memory. It would be a Happy New Year, a very Happy New Year, indeed!

On the fifth of April in 1880, Harlow and Hannah were married and nearly the entire town turned out to wish them well. There was music and dancing and plenty of food for everyone. Mary Louise sang at their wedding and James gave Hannah away. She felt like a renewed spirit regaling in such happiness. Nettie had made her dress, and that was the start of her new dress and tailor business. She and Mary had decided to start their own enterprise and Hannah was her first real buyer.

Not long before the wedding, Nettie had met a gentleman from Kansas in the cafe and the sparks flew. Walter Thompson was a wealthy cattleman contracting to bring cattle into the cavalry camps for the government. It was love at first sight for them both, and they were married six months after Hannah and Harlow had tied the knot.

Nettie and Walter left Silver City for his ten-thousand acre ranch in Coolidge, Kansas, in October. Nettie and Hannah tried to be happy for each other, but the sorrow in parting was difficult to bear. They were close as sisters, having shared so much in the past year in Silver City. Hannah promised to look after Mary, who would take over the dress and tailor shop as full owner. "I'm grateful to have a friend like you for Mary to look to if she needs anything," Nettie told Hannah. "You're very dear to her, you know. One day I know she'll be your daughter-in-law. I only wish I could come for the wedding, whenever it is," Nettie sighed. Too bad I couldn't have married a local man so I wouldn't have to leave my dearest friends."

It was a sad farewell when Nettie finally boarded the stage. Mary waved until it was out of sight, and James just held her close and watched the dust cloud roll away. Things were changing in Silver City.

Chapter 7

James was surprised at how bad the conditions were at the mine. He would come home exhausted and restless. He began spending more time with Sam, diligently prospecting for a strike of their own.

They had a claim on one small vein of silver and had some Mexicans working the claim. It paid average but James wanted more. He quit the mine and devoted his time to prospecting with Sam. The second claim was richer and near the site of the first one. When that one was going well he would sometimes go into the saloon in the evening, sit in on a game of poker and have a few drinks.

One night a cowboy by the name of John Dodson, from up Montana way, came into the saloon. He was with a bunch of Texans bringing cattle up from the border to be shipped out to points east. He had already received half his pay and heard Silver City was where you could find a good poker game.

After brief introductions, John took a seat and was dealt into the game. Unfortunately he was no match for James at the poker table, so after losing a few too many hands he decided to do a little cheating. A friend had shown him how to hold the ace back and use it when needed. When the pot was a good one and all bets were in, James was holding three jacks and sure his hand had won. John decided this was the time to use the ace, so he slipped it out of his sleeve.

James, sensing something was wrong when John had a low straight flush, called John on the hand. "I think you're a cheat!" James said glaring hard into John's eyes. With that, John jumped up and pulled a gun on James

and challenged him to prove
it. Everyone else at the table
was struck silent by surprise.

Since James couldn't
prove that John had cheated
with the ace up his sleeve, the
man walked out with a pot of
over five hundred dollars.

James would not forget
that John had done him dirt. It
tasted like gall on his tongue
and he went home seething.
He wasn't a vengeful man, but
he had a real problem with
dishonest poker players.

It was the fifteenth of
April in1882, when James and
Mary were finally married.
They had wanted to wait till
they had enough money saved
to buy a ranch and both had
worked hard to make their
dream come true. Mary sold
the dress shop so she could
devote herself to helping
James with the ranch.

The house was built and
a barn raised before winter set
in, as friends all rallied to
help. Jake and Peter shipped

them two hundred head of longhorns from Austin to get their herd started, as their wedding gift. James had grown tired of mining and decided he could ranch and be successful, thanks to Hans' training in Texas and his growing up on the ranch there.

A short time later, Mary got a letter from Aunt Nettie.

> *Dear Mary,*
>
> *My precious Walter has been taken ill and can't work like he used to. We were thinking maybe you and James might consider coming to Coolidge for a while to help with the ranch. I've told him all about James and he wants someone with ranching experience he can trust. No one fits that description better than your husband. We would love to have you come live here and see how you like Kansas.*

Please reply soon my love to you and James. Also greet Hannah for me. I miss her so much. Friends are more valuable than gold.

Love,

Aunt Nettie

After a family discussion at the cafe among Hannah, Harlow, James and Mary, it was decided that James and Mary would go to Kansas and do what they could for Aunt Nettie. Mary Louise was obviously unhappy about the decision. She enjoyed having Mary and James close by and was not anxious to see them leave, but she loved Aunt Nettie just as they all did, and knew she needed help now.

The Silver City Sheriff's son, Alfred accepted the job of ranch manager at James' and Mary's place and began preparing to move his family to the ranch. James and Mary had set about their own preparations to leave for Kansas post haste.

Three weeks after Mary had received Nettie's letter they were on their way. "Mary, don't you dare have a baby while you're gone," Hannah chided. "I want to help bring my grandchildren into this world myself!"

"You'll just spoil them," James teased. "That's my job!" Hannah exclaimed, laughing. "And I plan to enjoy doing it."

It had been a year and a half since Mary had seen her Aunt Nettie and she was anxious for their reunion. She and James took the Butterfield Stage to El Paso and boarded the train for Kansas. Making their way to their seats they both felt the weight of oncoming responsibilities at Aunt Nettie's.

They had only two hours between their stage arrival

and the train departure, barely enough time to get a bite at the cafe and freshen up a bit. Both were exhausted from the stage ride and mighty glad to be on the train. "I'm going to sleep," Mary told James. "Don't wake me till we get there!"

"That'll be quite a nap, Mary dear," James laughed. "I could use some shut-eye myself. Thank Heaven for trains!"

Chapter 8

When they arrived at the train station in Kansas they were met by the ranch foreman, Nestor Clay. He was an older, gray-haired man who walked with a noticeable limp. It was obvious to James that the ranch may be more than a man his age could manage alone, although he was a personable gent with a wide smile and bright blue eyes that seemed to light up at the sight of Mary and James.

"I'm Nestor, Walter's right-hand man," he told them as they shook hands and introduced themselves. "I'm mighty glad to see ya. My, ain't you the purtiest thing that's come to Kansas," he said smiling broadly at Mary. "Your Auntie has just talked and talked about you. She sure was right when she said you was a lovely gal."

Mary immediately liked Nestor and laughed gaily at his compliment. "Well, you just charmed her right off her feet there, Nestor," James told him, winking at Mary. "I kinda think she's a looker too, if ya know what I mean!"

"Oh, I can see trouble coming with you two!" Mary chided. "If you don't behave I'll have James do the cooking and you can peel potatoes!" That got a great laugh out of both men as they put the bags in the wagon and climbed in for the two-hour ride to the ranch.

When they came through the gate, which read "Tumbling T Ranch", Mary was in awe at the peaceful setting. It was a lovely place with the road to the house winding through an ancient orchard. Enormous old oak trees shaded the front yard and a little creek flowed placidly beneath them, then out toward the pastures and hills beyond. The house was a two-story, white with green shutters and a broad porch across the front.

Aunt Nettie appeared in the doorway before they were all the way to the hitching rail. She was calling to them and waving excitedly. The evening sun's rays glinted off her glasses and a breeze toyed with wisps of her graying hair. She looks good, Mary thought. Nestor pulled the buckboard up to the rail and James jumped down and gently helped Mary down, knowing how anxious she was for that first hug from her wonderful aunt.

While the women hugged and cried, as women tend to do at times like those, James brought their bags to the porch. Nestor took the wagon on around to the barn while the others all greeted one another.

"Oh, James," Aunt Nettie said, half laughing half crying. "I didn't mean to neglect you! Come give me a big hug! I'm just all a-twitter having you all here. Gracious, it seems like it's been such a long time. Don't you two look grand!"

She wiped the tears from her cheeks with her apron, then put her arm through Mary's and beckoned, "Come in, come in. Let's have something cool to drink and visit a spell.

The interior of the house was quite a sight for Mary to behold. Never had she seen a home so beautifully done. Rich draperies framed the windows, cherry wood with brocade furniture, and paintings and photographs everywhere. "This is exquisite! You live like a queen, Aunt Nettie," she said examining a small china figurine of a couple dancing.

At that moment a tall black lady with silver hair in a bun came through the door from the kitchen and asked Aunt Nettie what she would

like to serve her guests.
Mary's eyebrows raised as she
looked from Pauline to Aunt
Nettie. A maid, she thought to
herself. My aunt has a maid!

"Pauline, this is my
niece, Mary, and her husband,
James," Aunt Nettie said
introducing them. "This is
Pauline. She's a dear. She's
been with Walter since his
children were small and I
don't know how I would
manage without her."

Aunt Nettie took a seat
on the sofa and motioning to
Mary to come sit beside her,
told Pauline, "I believe we'll
have some of that fresh
lemonade with a few wafers,
Pauline. Not too much so as to
spoil our dinner, though."
Pauline disappeared and
reappeared with a tray of
fresh-squeezed lemonade and
some cookies and wafers. She
smiled broadly as she set the
tray on the table in front of
the sofa. "Ah'm so happy to
finally be meetin' y'all after

all yo' auntie has tole me. She ce'tainly think the sun shine fo' dis girl, she said.

"Thank you, Pauline," Mary replied laughing and blushing.

"I'm happy to meet you, too, and I thank you so much for helping Aunt Nettie with all this," she said waving her hand around the parlor. "There's a lot here to keep up, I'm sure."

"Yes'm," Pauline smiled. "But yo' auntie, she be a hard worker, too." With that she again disappeared into the kitchen. Mary was fascinated and gave Aunt Nettie a look of sheer awe.

Aunt Nettie just nodded, knowingly. "She's been wonderful; truly a blessing to this ranch," she smiled.

"Aunt Nettie, if you and the rest of you lovely ladies will excuse me for a while, I'd like to go out and see if I can find Walter or Nestor and take a look around the place,"

James said rising from his seat and nodding to them politely.

"Of course, James," Aunt Nettie smiled apologetically. "This woman-talk must be boring you to tears! You'll most likely find one of them out back in the shed, just beyond the garden. I'm sure you'd like to get familiar with the ranch and talk business, so go on along. When you hear the dinner bell, just come a-runnin'!"

James excused himself, then, and ambled out the back door and past the garden toward the shed. He was already duly impressed with the apparent size and success of the Tumbling T. The horses he saw in the corral were of fine quality, one of which was in the process of being broken by one of the hands.

He rapped on the shed doorway so as not to startle Nestor. "Say, Nestor. If you have some time, I'd sure like to take a look around and ask some questions," he offered.

"Why sure, son," Nestor nodded. "Let me just finish honin' this blade, then we'll go check on some cattle down in the lower pasture."

They saddled a couple of horses and rode east along a rutted lane that led into a small meadow where the creek flowed away from the ranch house and disappeared again in the distance. The grass was lush and there were a few willow and cottonwood trees along the creek. The cattle looked fatter than any James had ever seen before. "What breed of cattle are these?" James asked Nestor.

"White-faced Herefords a good meaty steer. They can stay out on pasture for weeks and endure the cold and windy temperatures of the Kansas winters without so much as blinkin'," Nestor replied gesturing toward some steers under the trees at the creek.

They rode on out a couple of miles to some low hills and an outcropping of rock. When they reached the top of the highest hill they looked out to the northeast and James saw grassy plains stretching out before him in all directions, dotted with a few trees here and there.

North of the hills a windmill drew water to a tank and was spinning lazily in the early evening breeze. Cattle were grazing in the distance along with a few horses. As the shadows grew longer across the prairie James could make out Pike's Peak, with it's snowcap shrouded by a few hovering clouds, off in the distance to the west.

James and Nestor rode along a fence line for a couple of miles, then turned west and rode past a line shack used when round-up time came in the fall. There was a corral and chute along with evidence of branding, which was done in mid-summer to mark the new calves. Faintly they heard the dinner bell ringing at the ranch house and turned their horses toward the south again.

Back at the ranch house James went in to wash up and saw that Mary had unpacked most of their belongings. She smiled as he came into the room. "Well, how do you like the place?" she asked as he kissed her softly.

"It's a fine spread, Mary," he told her, dipping his hands into the washbasin. "I'm anxious to talk with Walter and learn more about it. Nestor is a good man, but I can tell he is mighty grateful to have help."

As they came down the stairs they saw Walter at the door of the library. "James, Mary! I'm so sorry I couldn't be here when you arrived I had some business in town that just couldn't wait. How was your trip?" After exchanging a few words of greeting, Walter told them, "After dinner we'll sit and visit. Then perhaps James and I can talk about the business of running this cattle ranch."

Dinner was a spread to behold. The beef was the finest James and Mary had ever tasted. "We don't get beef like this in Silver City," James announced. "Ours is ready to make into latigo by the time it gets to the table!"

"Now James," Mary chided, "it's not THAT bad!"

"Compared to this," he countered, "that ain't even beef!" He took another helping of meat and rolled his eyes in sheer enjoyment.

"You know, I haven't been too well as of late," Walter told them. "Nettie, here, said you were the man I needed since you've been in the cattle business, where was it down Texas way?"

"Yes sir," James replied, "near Austin. But those were longhorns, down there."

"I think after you learn about these Herefords you'll find they are a hardy breed of cattle offering more meat per steer, and we have the best bulls money can buy to ensure wholesome breeding. Nestor needs help and I need to rest a spell.

"We can surely use a capable young man such as yourself to run this place like a fine tuned fiddle. I hope you'll agree to stay on."

"I'd be pleased and honored to give it a try, sir," James smiled, giving Mary a wink. "I think my wife would disown me if I didn't!"

They finished their dinner and sauntered out to the front porch where a cool breeze stirred and the last rays of sunlight were fading. A quarter moon came up over the horizon and seemed to be only a few miles away, big and yellow-white in the steel blue twilight sky. Walter motioned to them to take a seat and they visited until Mary could hardly keep her eyes open any longer.

"It's been a long day for us both," James apologized. "We're mighty pleased to be here, though, and we look forward to a wonderful summer with you and Aunt Nettie." They rose and left the porch and heard Nettie urging Walter to do the same. Tomorrow would come soon enough and they would need their rest. James was so elated that he couldn't get to sleep right away, with his mind stirring about all he had to learn. He was smart as a whip, there was no doubt, and his memory was strong and clear.

Sometimes, when he was least expecting it, that poker game with John Dodson would drift across his mind haunting him, and he would feel his blood heat up. He pushed that thought away sternly. For the time being he was happy to be in Kansas to help Walter and Aunt Nettie. They were such fine folks. John Dodson would have to wait.

Next thing he knew Mary was sprinkling droplets of water on his forehead. He opened his eyes to see the early morning sun on Mary's gleaming hair and her sweet smiling face. He reached out and took her hand and pulled her down to sit next to him. As she kissed him gently he thought about how lucky he was to have such a beautiful lady for his wife.

There was a knock at the door. "James," Nestor's voice called out. "Y'all might want to get on down there for breakfast, 'fore it's all gone!"

"I'm on my way," James called back pulling on his pants and boots as quickly as possible. Mary followed him out the door and down the stairs. The aroma of bacon, potatoes, fresh bread and coffee tugged at their stomachs.

"Mornin', Mary." Nestor smiled. "We got a big day today." He gestured to a chair across the table for James. "Got to go up to the northern boundary and check that fence line. Then we need to get a count of calves. Eat hearty. We've got a long ride ahead of us." To Nora, the cook, he said, "If you would, ma'am, pack us some vittles for lunch. We should be back by dinner time."

At the corral Nestor introduced James to the ranch hands. There were ten in all, good, hard-working men. They had all heard about James and welcomed him amiably. It was a busy place, the Tumbling T, and James knew it would be a big responsibility. He secretly hoped he was up to it. After all, Walter had made his fortune on this land and wouldn't want to see it fail now!

It was a perfect day. Mere wisps of cloud streaked the azure sky and the air was brisk and refreshing. James had never seen so many cattle in his life. There was a herd of over eight hundred steers and calves, with ten prize bulls, all of which had won blue ribbons at the fair. There was a herd of fifty horses, which were used for cutting and as packhorses, a few mules for field work, and draft horses that were used in hauling the hay wagons.

Nestor took James over to the south range where oat fields stretched as far as the eye could see. Blowing in the wind, the oats reminded James of a picture he had seen of the ocean and waves.

For nearly a month James rode out regularly with Nestor to learn the cattle operation and get familiar with the layout of the ranch. Walter was pleased to see how quickly James was picking up the reins. He felt at peace knowing that while he was ill the ranch was in good hands. With James and Nestor at the helm the Tumbling T would most certainly continue to prosper.

Following another trip to town to see the doctor, Walter was given the diagnosis of Consumption. He was getting weaker and knew he didn't have much time left. Breathing was becoming more and more difficult and he was no longer able to climb stairs or ride a horse.

Even short walks were too taxing to his lungs, so he was confined to staying around the house, which was not an easy thing for Walter Thompson. Here was a man who had been on the go all his life, working the ranch, running cattle to market, traveling, doing it all. It was a sad time for Nettie, too, seeing the man she adored be stricken with such a debilitating illness. He coughed and struggled so hard to breathe that it made Nettie's chest ache in sympathy. By September he was confined to bed and the end was drawing near.

Six months after James and Mary had arrived in Kansas, Walter died. Everything stood still on the ranch. Walter's children came to call and hundreds of friends he had made over the years sent their condolences.

The funeral parlor was so crowded that folks had to stand outside in the drizzling rain. James and Mary did all they could to help Aunt Nettie cope with the overwhelming response to Walter's death. It was nearly a week before the ranch was up and running again. Few words were spoken among the men as they went about their chores, and the women were tearful and subdued. Nettie took Walter's passing so hard that the doctor confined her to bed rest for a week.

Chapter 9

A month after Walter's death, Nettie began to regain her strength and spoke of how she was looking forward to Christmas. "It's my favorite holiday of the year and when this place is decorated it makes Mount Vernon pale in comparison!" she chuckled.

"I'll need everyone's help, as I intend to make it an unforgettable event. And you know, Mary," Aunt Nettie went on as they were putting away jars of pumpkin from the last of the fall harvest, "It would be mighty nice to have some little feet running around here. Christmas just isn't the same without children!"

Mary blushed and laughingly said, "Well, Aunt Nettie, it just so happens that there has been a surprise coming your way. We didn't want to say anything because you were mourning Walter's passing and were so ill, but after the first of January we are expecting a baby!"

Aunt Nettie was thrilled and hugged Mary so hard it made her head swim. "Oh my sweet girl, that is wonderful news! I only wish my dear Walter could be here to share it. He loved children so and often spoke of how he missed his own. I suppose Hannah knows?"

"Oh yes," Mary smiled. "I wrote and told her a month ago. "She's planning on coming right after New Year's. The holidays are so busy for her there, as she too, decorates like it was the Windsor Castle or something! She really can't get away until after the first. You should be hearing from her any day now as to her plans. She made me promise not to have her first grandchild without her there to help bring him into this world. Him or her, that is," she laughed.

"This is wonderful, Mary!" Aunt Nettie exclaimed. "I'll get to see my dearest friend and her new grandchild, too! Goodness, we have preparations to be made! This will be a most glorious event for everyone at the Tumbling T."

Aunt Nettie's energy seemed to double as she set about planning and getting ready for the holidays and the birth of the new baby. Not a thing was overlooked. She even had Pauline and Nora knitting baby clothes with her in their spare time, as they shared in all the excitement.

James seemed to fade in and out of the activities, as his work was consuming most of his time. Winter approached swiftly and much had to be done in readiness for the harsh cold weather ahead. The ranch was humming along, thanks to his knowledge and energy, and everyone was grateful for his abilities in the business.

On a cold, blustery day in January, Aunt Nettie sent a message to Doctor Moore that Mary was having some labor cramps, so he would be ready to come out to the house on short notice. The storm worsened and blinding snow was blowing. Mary feared the doctor wouldn't be able to come through the blizzard.

Nora, the cook, assured them she would be able to deliver the baby when Mary was ready, as she had delivered several in her lifetime. She was a lady in her fifties and had five children, all grown. Her husband had died of pneumonia just two years earlier and, since he and Walter had been good friends, she was offered the position as cook at the Tumbling T. She was happy to get the chance to have a nice place to live and work and she and her youngsters became like family to Nettie.

Nora was known all over the county for her delicious apple pies and strudel, which won blue ribbons every year at the fair. She was certain Mary was about due, since the day before Mary had been busy trying to mop the floor and clean the pantry. "Mary, I think tomorrow you'll have a new baby to take care of. You see, just before a baby is born, the mother has a burst of energy," Nora had told her.

"I'm hoping this will do it," Mary replied laughing. "I'm certainly ready for him to come...or...her!"

Nora was right as rain. During the night Mary awoke with a dull backache and just couldn't get comfortable. She didn't want to wake James, but about two in the morning she let go a scream and James lurched and fell right out of bed! "Mary, what is it?" James reached for Mary and held her as she hugged her pillow and moaned softly.

"James, you'd better go fetch Nora. I think it's about time." He ran down the stairs and through the house to Nora's room. Banging on her door, he called to her and began rambling on about Mary.

She knew what James was trying to tell her. "Slow down, James," Nora told him reassuringly. "Everything will be fine." She had already made a box of clean cloths ready and had put water on the stove when she went to bed in anticipation of the coming birth. Lights came on as she called to the other women. She hurried up the stairs with Nettie and Pauline at her heels.

James was a nervous wreck, first running up to the bedroom door to see if he could hear anything, then back to the kitchen for more coffee. When things got quiet behind the bedroom door

James stood there holding his breath, eyes wide, waiting for what would happen next. A baby's cry broke the silence and James laughed out loud in relief as Aunt Nettie came dashing out the door, running right into him.

On that morning, the eleventh of January in 1883, a bouncing baby boy was born to Mary and James. Outside the winds were howling and the snow was blowing, but inside was enough merriment to warm the Arctic Circle.

"Oh James! It's a beautiful baby boyl!" Aunt Nettie cried in delight. James' eyes got wider and the biggest grin on earth crossed his face.

"A boy?" he said in disbelief. "It's a BOY!!" He grabbed Aunt Nettie in an enormous bear hug, nearly crushing the poor woman.

"Go on in," she told him, "before you hurt somebody!" Laughing,

James went in and saw his son just as Nora was handing the baby to Mary.

"Oh, James, isn't he beautiful?" Mary whispered, smiling. She was tired, but had done very well in the birthing of the seven-pound baby.

"What are you going to call him?" Aunt Nettie asked them as she gazed fondly at the infant.

"We've decided on James," James told her. "The name has been in my family for a long time and it's always been given to the firstborn boy. He will be James Jesse Quigley."

He sat in a chair next to Mary, smiling with pride at mother and child. Nora patted him on the shoulder and he shook her hand and thanked her profusely for a job well done. As everyone retreated to leave them alone for a while, Nora suggested Pauline start a fresh pot of coffee.

"Miste' James Jesse, he

come jus' in time fo' breakfast!" she laughed deep in her throat. "He gonna be a fine boy, Miste' James!" And with a wink she closed the door and headed downstairs to the kitchen.

Daylight was breaking when James came down to join them all in the dining room. "They're sleeping like babies," he grinned. "I don't know how to thank all of you for all you've done."

"I think you and Mary done all the work, Miste' James," Pauline chuckled. "We jus' givin' it a home."

The storm subsided soon after sunup and the earth was covered in fresh, powdery snow. Everything looked so perfect and white. Not long after James had gone down to the tool shed to do some work Aunt Nettie hollered from the front door. "It's Hannah and Mary Louise!" They were coming in a buggy from town, waving and shouting to Aunt Nettie.

"You're just a few hours
late," Aunt Nettie told them
amid the hugs and tears of
welcoming. "He couldn't wait
another minute! Hannah, you
have a beautiful new
grandson."

Hannah was breathless.
"How's Mary?" she asked
removing her cloak and
heading for the stairs.

"Wonderful!" Aunt
Nettie told her gathering their
wraps. "She'll be thrilled to
see you. Mary Louise! I
hardly recognized you. My, oh
my! How you've grown!"

Hannah tapped lightly on
the door and entered at Mary's
beckoning. They hugged and
cried for a full five minutes
before Hannah went to the
cradle and took baby James in
her arms. "James Quigley, I'm
happy to meet you," she
smiled lovingly. "I'm your
grandmother Hannah." She sat
down in the rocking chair next
to Mary's bed and adored the
sleeping infant as the tears
trickled down her cheeks.

"I so wanted to be here

when he was born," she told Mary, gazing at his dark hair and long eyelashes. "But I guess little James had other plans. He looks like a Quigley, he does. No doubt about that!"

"He is a determined one," Mary acknowledged with a laugh. "I'm just glad you got here so quickly. I hope your trip wasn't too tiresome."

"Well," Hannah replied with a slight frown. "If it hadn't been for that storm..."

Just then Mary Louise entered the room and swiftly crossed the floor to Mary's bed. "Mary, congratulations!" she exclaimed giving her a hug. "May I?" she motioned to Hannah to take the baby from her arms. Mary Louise was glowing with pride.

"I'm an aunt!" she declared spinning around slowly holding baby James close.

"Mercy yes!" Hannah said with feigned exasperation. To Mary she said, "And she's been singing a song about it all the way here!" They all laughed and James Jesse just slept through soundly while the three women caught up on their lives.

Nettie appeared at the door a while later and offered Hannah and Mary Louise some tea and cookies in the parlor while Mary rested. "We'll come back up after you have a nap," Hannah told Mary, smoothing her hair back from her face. "I'm so proud of you, and so thrilled with that darling grandson. I can't wait to see James!"

In the parlor, Nettie motioned to Hannah and Mary Louise to sit by the fire and inquired about news of Silver City. Nestor came in and she introduced him to the women. "James will be here in an hour or so. Got a cow down in the north pasture. He and a couple of hands went up there to tend to her," he told them, rubbing his hands together near the

fireplace to warm them.
"How's that baby doing?" he
asked Nettie.

"Fine," Nettie smiled.
"You'd better pick out a
spirited horse for that boy!
He'll be ready to ride in no
time!"

Pauline came into the parlor
to announce that dinner would
be ready soon and ask if they
should wait for James. "Yes,
please," Nettie told her. "We
want to all sit down together,
the first time in a long time.
Maybe Mary will feel up to
coming down and joining us
for a little while if she is
rested," she smiled hopefully.

It was after dark when
James came in. Shedding his
coat and hat he was already
calling to Hannah from the
back door. "Mother, Mary
Louise! Hello!" His eyebrows
went up as he caught his first
glance of Mary Louise. He
swept Hannah into his arms,
then reaching for Mary
Louise, said, "And who is this

gorgeous young blossom?"

Laughing and crying, Mary Louise wrapped her arms around his waist and hugged him tight. "I've missed you so much!"

"I've missed you too," he told her. "I've missed both of you very much. How is Harlow doing?" he asked Hannah. "I want to hear all about the cafe and saloon, what's happening in Silver City, everything!"

"Let's eat," Nettie said. "We can visit during dinner. James, see if Mary feels up to coming down for dinner. We can put the baby's cradle near the fireplace in the dining room to keep him cozy." Well, that was the noisiest dinner the Tumbling T had ever witnessed. Everyone seemed to talk at once, but everyone heard everything everyone else said. It was a rare and joyful occasion for everyone there.

Hannah and Mary Louise

stayed for two weeks doting on baby James and visiting with Mary, James, and Nettie. The time flew by and they enjoyed every minute.

"Why are visits always over before you're ready to leave?" Mary Louise said tearfully as they were packing their things to leave.

"Nettie," Hannah offered, "why don't you think about coming back to Silver City again? It's grown into a fair size town now and business is good there. Everyone asks about you, and if you're coming back. And I can always use help at the cafe."

"I'll think about it, Hannah," Nettie replied thoughtfully. "Since Walter died it has been almost too much for me to take care of this place. I don't know what I would have done without James and Mary. They have been such a blessing to me."

"Do come back, Aunt Nettie," Mary Louise pleaded. "Then you can hear me play the piano and sing. Someday I want to do it onstage, maybe in San Francisco or New York!" Nettie hugged her tight and agreed to think it over.

It was a tearful good-bye. Hannah didn't want to leave the new grandson behind, but she knew she had to get back to Harlow. He would be pulling his hair out after another week of her being gone, she was sure. It was a big job running both the saloon and cafe. She thanked God often that he was a good and capable partner, in every way.

A couple of evenings later, at dinner, Nettie asked James what he thought about her moving back to Silver City. "Well, I reckon it's grown some, but it was always a nice town, and you've got to admit, the winters are considerably easier. 'Sides, you've got family and friends there. Seems to me, it would be more like home to you."

"Your mother and sister miss you terribly, and are going to be longing for that grandson," Aunt Nettie smiled ruefully. "They told me they would like me to consider coming back and I've been giving it some thought. Joe Merrill has offered to buy this place a number of times but, of course, Walter wouldn't think of it when he was alive.

Now he's gone and it's just more than I need. I miss my friends and if Joe would give me a fair price for this place, I think I might sell. Nora would most likely come with me, but Pauline has kin in Missouri and would rather go there, I think. Anyway, it would take a few months to get things in order once I do have an offer. Will you and Mary stay and help me, James?"

"Why, sure, Aunt Nettie," he told her taking her

aging hand in his. "We'll do whatever needs to be done, and then we'll all go home to Silver City. It's a fine place to raise a son, and we'd all be together there," he smiled to Mary. And so it was agreed, they would all return to Silver City before fall.

Chapter 10

In the late 1800's rail transportation in the West was expanding rapidly and becoming better regulated. Since travel and shipping of goods was faster and easier, folks were moving in that direction in great numbers. Many were anxious for a new start in the western frontier since a number of the Indian tribes had been removed to reservations. In New Mexico, the Lincoln County War had subsided and Billy the Kid and the Regulators were no longer running rampant since his death in 1881.

The Apaches were sent to Florida after Geronimo's capture in 1886, thus reducing the Indian threat against settlers in the New Mexico and Arizona Territories. A German by the name of Gottlieb Daimler had developed the gas motor with a crank start which, in the future, would enable automobiles to swarm the continent, and Grover Cleveland had just become the President of the United States. It was a time of rapid change and progress in the West.

Major changes were taking place in James and Mary's lives as well. As they had planned following Walter's death, they were helping Aunt Nettie pack and prepare for the move to Silver City before autumn. The Tumbling T Ranch was sold and half of the cattle were to be shipped to market by the end of the month.

The remainder of the stock was to stay with the ranch to continue the success of breeding. Nestor had agreed to stay on with the new owners. For him it was too late in life to make such a drastic move. He was used to Kansas and preferred to remain in familiar surroundings. His knowledge of the operation of the Tumbling T had earned him a position as overseeing consultant, sort of a supervising foreman without so much manual labor.

He was pleased as punch. James was happy too, as he had grown extremely fond of Nestor and wanted to see him satisfied with the changes that were taking place.

Letters from Hannah were filled with anticipation

at James' and Mary's return to Silver City, as well as that of Nettie. The ranch James and Mary had left in Alfred's care was doing well, but James had been entertaining thoughts of looking into new mines in the area. Ranching was an arduous business and often kept the men from their families. James was thinking on being home every evening to enjoy his wife and children as his family grew.

"Do you think we should tell Nettie about the new baby coming?" Mary was just starting to show her pregnancy at about four months along.

"Yes, I think she should know. She could be of help to you after we get back to Silver City," James replied thoughtfully. Nettie was delighted to hear about the new baby. Jimmy was walking now and had plenty of energy. Mary would certainly be grateful to have Nettie's help.

"I'm so glad Nora has decided to come along. She'll be such a good companion for you and she's so fond of Jimmy. I think she would miss him terribly if she stayed here," Mary told Aunt Nettie as they carefully packed the breakables from the parlor hutch.

"They have taken a shine to one another, that's for sure!" Aunt Nettie laughed. The evening before they were to leave, Aunt Nettie set about to provide a suitable farewell dinner for all the ranch employees.

It was quite a sumptuous affair. There was beef, wild turkey, and lake trout, and every vegetable in season from the garden to tempt the most discriminating palate. Aunt Nettie and Nora had outdone themselves, baking apple, Cherry, and gooseberry pies. It was a banquet fit for a king.

"I can't tell you how

difficult it is to leave all of you," Aunt Nettie told them after grace had been said over the meal. "You have been far more than just Walter's employees. You are the Tumbling T Ranch! You have taken me in and made me your friend, and I am so grateful for all you have done for me....for all of us. I know I speak for Walter too, when I say that you are a wonderful example of what this country represents.

"May God bless each and every one of you, and I pray our trails will meet again one day, if not here, then in the Great Beyond!" And with tears trickling down her cheeks, she raised her glass of apple wine and toasted them with love and admiration.

Little Jimmy was the pride of the ranch, and everyone wanted to hug him or have him sit on their laps before the evening was done. "Mommy," he said as Mary tucked him into bed, "I sure love everybody!!" Mary's eyes filled with tears as she said bedtime prayers with her son, and together they thanked the Lord for the fine folks they had grown to love so dearly at the Tumbling T.

The following morning Nestor drove them to the train station where they bade him a tearful farewell. The train would take them all the way to Deming, New Mexico, this time, making the stage ride much shorter, a blessing to Mary in her condition.

James was looking forward to getting back to Silver City.
He had written to Sam, his old prospecting friend, to learn of any new ore strikes and get information about a new silver mine that was to have opened about forty miles south of Silver City, at Gage. Sam had told him it was a good operation and they were looking for experienced men for foreman positions.

James had approached

Mary with the prospect of selling the ranch in Silver City to Alfred and working at the mine in Gage. He said they could have a nicer home and he would be able to spend more time with the family. She was agreeable, so they were looking forward to finding or having a new home built that would accommodate their growing family.

It was a long trip for Mary, in spite of the blessing of rail transportation. She was exhausted after the past week's activities and packing to leave the Tumbling T. It had all been a bit too much for her. Aunt Nettie and Nora kept Jimmy occupied during the trip so that she could get some sorely needed rest.

"Mary, be sure to make an appointment with the Doctor when we get to Silver City," Nora suggested. "Maybe he can recommend a tonic to get some strength and energy back into your system for you and that new baby."

Harlow met the stage when they arrived in Silver City. He had a wagon ready to load all their baggage and take them to the house.

"It's so good to see you," he hugged the women and Jimmy.

Slapping James on the back he said, "Hannah, and Mary Louise are so excited to see all of you." With a grin he leaned toward Mary and in a loud whisper said, "Mary, I think they are itching to spoil that little Jimmy fella!"

When they got to the house, Hannah was waiting anxiously on the front porch. "Come in...oh do come in!" she exclaimed amid the hugs and tears of joy.

"Let me see that young man," she motioned toward Jimmy, who was shyly hanging onto Mary's skirt with eyes wide in wonder. "Mercy sakes! You're near full-grown!" she laughed hugging the squirming boy. "And Mary, there's another blessing on the way? How wonderful! This time I'll be at the birthing, for sure!" Shooing everyone inside, she pulled Mary aside and suggested she take the room downstairs so she could go rest from the trip before dinner.

"Oh, Hannah," Mary replied tearing up, "I'm so grateful to be here with you again. I am tired, but I'll be fine. Please don't worry, his baby is in safekeeping," she smiled patting her blossoming tummy. They hugged, then Harlow took Mary's and James' things into the front bedroom and left her to rest a while.

Meantime, everyone was in the parlor, and all talking at once. Mary Louise was ecstatic at having James home again. She sat glued to his side, admiration filling her eyes, while he answered hers and Harlow's questions and told them his plans. Hannah and Aunt Nettie were catching up on the local news and making plans for the remainder of the week.

At dinner that evening, James approached Hannah and Harlow with the request that Mary stay with them while he looked into a job down at the mine at Gage. He told them of his plan to sell the ranch outside of Silver City to Alfred, the Sheriff's son, who had done such a fine job looking after the place while they were in Kansas. Alfred was all too eager to buy, so a fair deal had tentatively been cut quickly by telegraph a month before they left the Tumbling T, and both parties were very satisfied.

"I'm in a position to look for something that will allow me to be with my family more and provide a nicer home than the place out at the ranch," James told them. "What do you think, Harlow? Do you know much about that mine over there?"

"Could be a good opportunity, James," Harlow told him as he reached for another helping of greens. "I hear it's a good strike, so they should be operating for a while. As a foreman you ought to draw a good wage."

"If I can't find a suitable house, do you mind if Mary stays here till we can have one built? I would stay down at the miners' bunkhouse and come up on my days off," James offered.

"It's fine with us," Hannah smiled at Mary. "Besides, I intend to help deliver *this* grandchild! Jimmy will be a big help around here, too," she winked at Jimmy. He had warmed up quickly to his grandmother Hannah and a bond was already growing strong between them.

Mary Louise didn't appear too happy that James

would be moving again so soon. "Cheer up, little sis," he grinned. "I'll be around often enough to aggravate you some!"

Mary wasn't all that excited about James' plan to be away so much either, but she knew she was in no shape to travel any more until after the birth. Especially, considering they would be going into such isolated country, she had readily agreed to stay with Hannah.

Chapter 11

James rode out the next morning in the direction of Gage. It was barely an hour after sun-up and the desert smelled of creosote while a slight breeze toyed with the mesquite and palo verde trees. The landscape was less than attractive.

Besides the scattered trees, there was cholla, prickly pear cactus with it's bright reddish fruit, and yucca. There were no outstanding features except for a few cottonwood trees wherever water lay beneath the surface in some wash or stream bed.

He had to travel about fifteen miles south to a place called Cow Springs. It had been used as a Mexican watering hole many years before and was known then as Ojo de la Vaca (eye of the cow). When New Mexico was declared a territory it became a stop for the Butterfield Stage line, which was later taken over by Wells Fargo.

The Apaches caused continual problems until the treaty with Cochise. After that only the Mescalero bands frequented the area, and after Geronimo's capture they were rarely seen except when riding through with a stolen horse or two.

From there it was another twenty-five miles of the same terrain to the location of the Gage mining operation. James arrived at the mine shack late in the afternoon where he was met by the owner of the mine, Cliff Hart.

Cliff was a pleasant man in his late forties with a round, ruddy face and booming voice. "James good to meet you! Russ mentioned you would be coming by. Tell me what you're looking for and where you've worked before."

Russ, the chief of operations at the new mine, had given him a great recommendation. James knew him from when they had both worked at the Gold Hill mine in White Water outside Silver City. He told Cliff of his desire to be a foreman and summarized about his work at the Gold Hill, as well as the responsibilities he'd had at running the Tumbling T Ranch in Kansas.

"How 'bout we take a tour around the mine," Cliff suggested, slapping James on the back. "It's doing quite well and the grade of silver is good. I think we're about to hit a good solid vein of ore with, maybe, some gold in it too. You got a family?"

James told him about Mary expecting, and little Jimmy in Silver City. "We've put up some small houses for the miners and their families to rent." They ain't big and fancy, but they'll do till you get something bigger built. Not much to choose from that's already built, as Gage is still a booming town."

After the tour they returned to the guard shack. "So, what do ya think? Interested?" Cliff said seating himself on an empty explosives crate. "We can sure use a good foreman."

"Looks good to me, anything I need to know that you haven't told me?" James asked looking around the area again.

"Well, James, be sure and carry your gun with you all the time. You never know when a rattler will be under some timbers or rock. And sometimes a renegade Apache may try and steal your horse. You can just scare them off with a shot or two. The Mescaleros are still scattered around the area, but the Chiricahuas are on the run between Arizona and Mexico, so they don't give us much trouble now. Seems General Crook is pretty hot on Geronimo's trail. Keeps things quieter around here," Cliff nodded. "It's a growing town and we sure do want to have folks like you to help it grow. So, how about starting tomorrow morning, James?"

James sidestepped so as to avoid another slap on the

back. "That sounds fine. Where's the miner's bunkhouse so I can go get settled?"

"Right along that road about a mile, just over the hill," Cliff motioned to the east. "You'll see it on the left under some cottonwoods. Just put your horse in the corral. It's safe enough. There's always someone on guard to keep the place secure. Gotta be careful of the thievin' redskins!"

The country was wild with Indians, rattlesnakes, and cactus. It was hot as hell in the summer and colder than the devil in the winter. It wasn't attractive, not the least bit scenic, and James didn't know how Mary would react to the idea of living in Gage, but the job was good and pay was better than average, about two and a half bucks a day for a foreman.

There were about seventy-five people living in

Gage, mostly miners, but it had potential other than the view. There was already a good little cafe, a mercantile, a small hotel and saloon, and a church. At least one could counter balance the other.

James went into town to take a look at the houses the mine had built for its staff, which included foremen. There were about two-dozen nice houses that the first miners had built on the outskirts of the town, a few smaller houses in town, a sprinkling of shanties along the wash, and the mine-owned houses. These houses perched on a low rise at the east end of town. Each had three rooms, not much space in any of them, and a small porch on the front.

After what Mary had become accustomed to, this was considerably less attractive. James wasn't sure how she would accept this but, then, Mary was peaceable and rarely complained about anything. At least, this time they would have the house to themselves, rather than living with someone else, as it seemed they had done almost ever since their marriage.

Jimmy wouldn't be ready for school for a couple more years, so there would most likely be a schoolhouse by then. At the moment, school for the few children in town was being conducted in one of the mine-owned houses. It wasn't a paradise, but it was better than some mining towns that had sprung up in the territory. Many weren't much more than shantytowns with a name. When the mines played out, the miners just migrated to the next strike wherever they could get hired on.

It was a rough life for those who just worked in the pits or underground, and dangerous as well. Mining labor conditions and pay for the miners varied throughout the country, rarely being suitable. Regardless of what ore was being mined, many mines were built hurriedly and haphazardly, without a great deal of consideration given to the safety of the miners.

Some new laws were being enacted to regulate these factors, but were slow to be implemented by the mine owners. Enforcement was weak, at best. It was a risky, dirty, and tough business, but improvements were being made gradually.

Throughout the next month James worked hard at learning the ropes at the new mine. He was a responsible and conscientious young man determined to do well at whatever he attempted. His integrity and efforts to improve the conditions for the miners caught the attention of Cliff and Russ.

They were only too happy to have him as a foreman. Every other week he would get a couple of days off so he could go to Silver City and see Mary and Jimmy. Mary was getting close to the baby's due date and feeling the heat of the late desert summer.

Hannah was a blessing, as were Aunt Nettie and Nora, in caring for Jimmy so Mary could rest when needed. It was an exhausting pregnancy and the doctor was keeping a close eye on her. He insisted she rest as much as possible.

Jimmy was a curious and rambunctious child who wanted to try everything. Growing up, for him, was truly an adventure and he certainly was giving it his all. It was a full time job just keeping track of him. Aunt Nettie and Nora cared for him most of the time, as Hannah still had the cafe to run.

Jimmy loved to go into town with Grandma Hannah and "help" her at the cafe. Mary Louise would play tunes on the piano in the saloon and was teaching him to sing along with her. Everyone in town knew him and got a kick out of what a lively and good-natured boy he was.

On the fifteenth of September in 1884, Mary gave birth to Charles, with Hannah in attendance. He was a small baby, and a welcome addition to James' family. The doctor said he was quite healthy despite his being small. "He'll grow, Mary," Doctor Drake told her. "I assure you, I've not yet seen one that didn't!"

James was elated at having another son. "I'm going to have all sorts of help when these fellas get grown!"
Jimmy was ecstatic at having a new little brother. It was all Mary could do to keep him from grabbing Charlie and carrying him off someplace to play. Jimmy spent the next couple of weeks with Aunt Nettie and Nora, or Grandma Hannah and Mary Louise, until Mary got

her strength back.

That pregnancy had taken a lot out of her, what with moving from Kansas and all. She missed James and was anxious to reunite the family. James had secured a mine-owned house for them in Gage and was getting it ready for them to move into shortly after Thanksgiving. Hannah had made them promise not to move before that. She wanted her family there to revel in the holiday together.

Thanksgiving was a family extravaganza. Hannah went all out to see that it was an event to remember. The cafe and saloon were festooned in a harvest-time theme and there was enough food for half the territory. Family and close friends enjoyed a day of feasting and fun that everyone would recall for years thereafter. James couldn't eat enough of all the wonderful food that had been prepared.

"My horse is going to think he's carrying a ton of ore when I get on him tomorrow!" he declared, rubbing his satisfied stomach.

"When I get the food packed for you to take with you, he'll have no doubt!" laughed Hannah. "Just don't get ambushed. I need the customers to come to the cafe!"

Finally, the first week in December, James and Mary were packed and the wagon loaded for their move to Gage. Jimmy ran from Hannah to Mary Louise, then to Aunt Nettie and Nora saying, "Bye, love you!" again and again, until they finally lifted him up to the wagon to get started for Gage.

"Don't forget, Mary," Hannah smiled through her tears. You be here by the twentieth so we can get ready for the Christmas of the century!"

"We'll be here. Jimmy

won't let me forget, I'm sure!"
Mary shouted as the wagon
pulled away and they all
waved to each other.

James had tried to
prepare Mary for her
transition to the mine-owned
house, but she simply told
him she was only too happy
just to have a place of their
own to call home, again and
be together in it. She had
fully recovered from Charlie's
birth and was in high spirits
as they made their way across
the desert to their new house
in Gage. Jimmy was fidgety
with anticipation at seeing
where they would live next.
He loved adventure and
making new plans with his
mother and father.

It didn't take Mary long
to make the little house a
home. Jimmy was in the midst
of everything, helping with
what he could, and loving and
caring for Charlie. He would
talk to the baby as if it were
his son, explaining everything
in a very grown-up way, and

it kept Mary amused as she listened to her precocious son. She met the ladies in her neighborhood quickly, as the miners' wives were always pleased to welcome a new family. There were plenty of other children for Jimmy to play with and Charlie was one of the newer babies, so he got plenty of attention, too.

One morning James went out to get some wood for the fire and as he picked up a piece of wood, a rattlesnake struck at him. He jumped back, drew and fired his gun instantly, hitting the snake in the head. It wasn't uncommon to see snakes, but this one was the biggest James had ever seen. It measured almost six feet in length and had eight rattles, which denoted an age of about eight years.
Nestor would have been proud of James shooting like that. Nestor had been like a father to James at the Tumbling T Ranch. They would sit and talk for hours,

James listening intently to the many stories of Nestor's childhood and later years. He had been a gunsmith in Ohio before moving to Kansas, and was a crack shot. He could fast draw and hit just about any target dead center.

"Nestor, I'd sure like to learn to do that fast draw and shoot like you do," James had told him one day when they were in the shed waiting out a rainstorm. Nestor was only too happy to comply, and he had set up a target range a short distance from the stock corral where they could go and shoot when they could find the time.

"Son," Nestor had told James, "I've got one piece of advice for you. Never draw your gun on a man unless you plan on shooting him." James told Nestor about shooting the two men in Texas that had broken into his mother's house.

"You were lucky,"

Nestor had told James. "Those were some pretty tough characters. Must have been your lucky day boy. I even heard about that incident up here in Kansas, that those sidewinders were shot and killed by a young feller protecting his mother and sister."

It was a way of life and in the West guns were the law but that, too, was changing. So James had learned to be quite handy with his piece and he practiced when he could to keep his edge keen in case he was ever called to defend himself or his family. It was a skill that was necessary in the territory where life was precariously lived. Unfortunately both bad and good men carried and used guns as a means of getting what they wanted or keeping what they had.

Chapter 12

Aunt Nettie had bought a cozy little house on a hill overlooking the valley just west of Silver City. Nora was happy to be there with her and thrilled to be away from the inclement weather of Kansas. So grateful was she for the milder weather that she didn't mind the warmer summers at all. She had told Nettie the small amount of snowfall they saw in the winters was just enough to get her in the mood for Christmas.

"I love to see it on the mountains, but not deep on my back step!" she declared as she rolled out yet another piecrust. She still baked her apple pies, but now they were for the soldier camp and for Hannah's cafe. She was already well known in the area for her superb baked goods. Strudel was a specialty with her, and her apple tarts were in constant demand. She and Nettie were satisfied and happy living near Silver City.

Mary Louise came to visit often, as she was so fond of them both. They adored her, too, and were very impressed with her singing and dancing talent. She had become a beautiful young lady with hopes and dreams of going to New York to school for dance and voice lessons.

Hannah had told her about living in the big city, with the hope of discouraging her from going so far away, but Mary Louise would not be deterred. She had been singing and dancing in the saloon for a few years now and was ready to move on to a real stage. Whenever she would perform in the saloon, Hannah was always watching warily.

The men loved Mary Louise, sometimes a little too much. She was a feisty gal and quite sure of herself. She had no time for the local boys. "They are so young acting," she would say wrinkling her nose in disgust.

Whenever she could, she would run down to the theater just past the center of town to see Rose, the star performer. Rose was thrilled to have Mary Louise as her protege and would let her put on some of her dresses, get on the stage and dance and sing her heart out while Rose played the piano and coached her. Rose would tell her stories about what life was like in the big city of New York where the lights would burn all night and fancy carriages took rich people around town.

Mary Louise knew just what she wanted and there was no dissuading her. Hannah knew it wouldn't be long till Mary Louise would be saying farewell to Silver City and would turn her determined chin toward the glamour of New York. She could only pray that it would be the right thing for Mary Louise, who simply had no doubt.

As planned, Christmas was an even greater affair than Thanksgiving had been. Everything was decorated. Hannah even wore decorations in her hair and as jewelry. Packages were piled high under the tall blue spruce that had been brought down from the Mogollon Rim especially for the occasion.

James had brought his family up from Gage to Silver City, but had been asked to return to work until noon of Christmas Eve. The boys were kept busy from the moment they arrived. Jimmy had strung berries and popcorn until he couldn't eat or stand the sight of any more! His excitement was overflowing and contagious to everyone he knew. Charlie was still too tiny to understand any of the festivities, but he gurgled and cooed at all the colorful decorations and for all the family, who simply melted at his impish smile.

All the women and

Harlow had done an extraordinary job tending to customers, decorating, cooking, and selling baked goods. Hannah's cafe did a healthy business that day, and Hannah was exhausted but happy. They all went to church on Christmas Eve, and with lighted candles sang carols and thanked the Lord for a good year. Aunt Nettie had made a beautiful wreath in memory of Walter and it had been placed on the door of the church in his honor.

Afterwards they went to Hannah's again for cranberry punch, tea, coffee and pastries. As the hour grew late Mary and James, who were staying with Hannah as usual, tucked the boys into bed, then said goodnight as all the guests departed. Soon everyone was asleep, some anxiously awaiting the mysterious visit of a spry elf named Santa.

Christmas Day was organized chaos. Everyone

gathered at the saloon after a light breakfast and sang carols. Aunt Nettie stepped forward to share her love and gratitude to all in attendance, and to the Good Lord above, for all the blessings throughout the year. She paused, turned her gaze upon the beautiful tree, then lifting her eyes skyward softly said, "Merry Christmas, Walter. It must be some celebration where you are!" After a moment of silence everyone applauded and wished Walter a Merry Christmas.

Hannah was next to speak and thanked everyone for all they had contributed to hers and Harlow's lives throughout the year. She expressed the joy of having two incomparable grandsons and so many blessings from above. One by one, they went around the room, each giving a brief thanks for family, good health and prosperity. The gifts were then handed out by Mary Louise and

James, the children being first and most impatient to receive theirs. No love had been spared in the gift giving. Everyone was having a wonderful time, especially watching Jimmy run from one person to the next to see what they got as they opened their gift.

It was cacophony, the sound of a happy gathering of family, and it was wonderful. The food was beyond description, only to say no one left the table hungry, but rather most folks over-indulged. James claimed he had actually eaten himself into pain, and Mary Louise suggested they have some music and dance it off.

"Oh Mother!" Mary Louise exclaimed. "I think Jesus would *love* to have dancing and singing at His birthday party!" With that everyone laughed and applauded, then began to dance as she played a lively tune on the piano.

No one would ever forget that Christmas. It was the warmth of family, music of laughter, and joy of contentment that would carry them through the trials and hardships that would come in a future they could not see. Such is the way of life. Strength comes from the love of family and friends, and the good Lord above.

Chapter 13

Spring came early in southern New Mexico that year, in 1885. James and Mary had been giving much thought to building a house on the outskirts of Gage. Mary simply asked that it have somewhat of a view, preferably from a hill, so she didn't feel so much like she lived in a squatters' town.

She wasn't the uppity sort, but Gage wasn't a pretty place and James fully understood. He'd seen prettier places, but the income from the mine was good and he hoped he could build a nice house that would make Mary happier to be there.

The blessing was they weren't terribly far from Silver City, so Mary and the boys were able to go for a visit every couple of months, which was a welcome respite from the dreariness of Gage. At least there was an actual town in Silver City, with some culture and diversity. It was also more scenic as you traveled a little north or west toward the pines at the foot of the Mogollon Rim. It was a hot day in July as James, Mary, Jimmy, and Charlie rode in the buggy to pay a visit to Hannah and Nettie.

When they arrived at Hannah's, she came out to greet them. Mary noticed her eyes were red and swollen, and elbowed James to draw his attention. "Mother, you look as though you've been crying. Is something wrong?" he asked her.

"We just put Harlow in the hospital this morning," she said sniffing and pulling out her hanky. "The doctor thinks he may have had a heart attack. This morning he was in the saloon closing out from last night. He hollered at me to come help him, next thing I knew he was laying on the floor holding his chest.

Oh James, I'm so afraid!"

James held Hannah tight as she began to cry again. He knew she had already lost two husbands and he sure didn't want to see her hurt again. Mary shooed the boys into the house and they all went into the kitchen for some cool lemonade.

"Mary, leave the boys here with Mary Louise and we'll take mother to the hospital," James suggested. Mary Louise was only too happy to have the boys to herself for a while. She hugged her mother, then James ushered the women out to the buggy.

They met Nettie and Nora at the hospital, all having arrived at the same time. "How are you holding up?" Nettie asked Hannah.

"Not as well as I should, I expect. I'm so glad all of you are here. I am so scared. I just can't lose Harlow," and she began to cry again.

"There, there, mother. The doctors will do their best for him." James said reassuringly as he held her close.

They entered the cool dimness of the hospital and walked to the main waiting area. A nurse approached them and took Hannah by the arm. "I'm so sorry to have to tell you this, Mrs. Walsh. Your husband died about a half hour ago. He had another heart attack. There was just nothing anyone could do to help him."

Hannah turned white as a ghost, and as she turned to say something to James, she fainted. James scooped her up into his arms and the nurse was already motioning them into a room where a bed was ready. It was simply too much for Hannah to take. The nurse brought smelling salts and when Hannah came around, James saw the bewildered look on her face.

"I'm taking you home and putting you to bed," he told her. Mary and Nettie will be there to look after the cafe and saloon. You need to rest. I can't risk losing you!"

"James, I want to see Harlow once more before I leave," she tried a half smile. "He wouldn't want to be left alone like that."

James helped her to her feet and, hanging on tightly to each other, they followed the nurse down the hall and into the room where Harlow was lying. He had a peaceful look on his face, and Hannah took his hand and kissed it. "Harlow, I'm going to miss you terribly," she said as she sat down on the bed beside him.

James wanted to leave her alone for a few minutes, so motioning to Mary and Nettie, they stepped out of the room. The moment they were in the hall, James sat down on one of the chairs and let the tears flow. Mary and Nettie put their arms around him and they all wept together. The family was losing one of its finest members and the sorrow was overwhelming.

After the funeral James had to get back to the mine. He hated having to leave Hannah, but he knew she was strong and would survive, as she always did, somehow. They said farewell and hugged for a long moment before Hannah told him, "Go on now. You have a life to attend to, and so do I. Come visit again soon, but in the meantime you just take good care of yourself and that precious family. Nettie and Nora will be here till I have to kick them out! I love you all so much."

Silver City was a town full of good-hearted people, for the most part. Before the week was out Hannah had hired Joe Mullett to run the saloon.

He had been a saloon owner in the town of Hanover before the mine played out. Ghost towns were becoming almost as numerous as the boomtowns, while mining companies hit one shallow strike after another. Gage was still operating and doing well. Seemed there was more to that desert than just cactus and sagebrush.

It was a hot summer and Mary and the boys frequented Silver City whenever possible. It was a couple of degrees cooler there, and if you drove up to Pinos Altos it was even cooler. They would go on picnics up into the foothills to the northwest of town and sit under the pines and enjoy a cool breeze as they gazed out across the shimmering desert.

Occasionally they would see an antelope or deer as the shadows grew long in the late afternoon, and the boys would chase them as far as they could before being called back. They loved the grace and fleetness of the animals and kept asking James if they could catch one for a pet.

Finally cooler weather came with autumn. Nettie had been ill with a bronchial condition, and although the cough lingered, she was feeling better and back at the cafe helping Hannah. Hannah had slowed down some, not that many noticed, but Nettie and Nora did. They did their best to take up the slack so the cafe and saloon could run smoothly. Joe Mullett turned out to be a true blessing. An honest and hard-working man, he was, and he had helped Hannah immensely.

Autumn turned into winter and the holidays were only slightly subdued with the loss of Harlow. Hannah insisted on doing things as they always had. "Harlow would be beside himself if he thought we didn't celebrate with joy because of him! He will be right here with us every minute.

"I feel his presence so often and talk to him when I feel it. I know he is always nearby. We must carry on as if he were still here among us in person. That's how he would have it, and that's how it shall be," she told Mary and James when they had brought the boys into town for Halloween to go to a costume party.

Those boys of James' were Hannah's joy overflowing. She was the apple of their eyes too, and they spent as much time as possible helping her at the cafe or sitting on the sofa listening to her lilting voice as she read them stories.

Mary Louise was considered one of the stars in the sky, as far as Jimmy and Charlie were concerned. She taught them games, songs, and dances, and they adored her. Such loved and loving children they were! Any one of the family would have stolen them for keeps! They were rarely seen crying. Tears were turned into laughter as quickly as you could say Johnny-jump-up!

Christmas, that long-awaited magical time, was finally approaching and the excitement mounted by the hour. Jimmy would burst from Hannah's kitchen with flour on his hands and face beaming that he had just made Santa's cookies. Charlie sat in the high chair and ate.....everything. Everyone was bustling about getting the cafe and saloon ready and preparing for the grand Christmas Day celebration.

James had been making toys for his two sons, spending long evenings in the mine workshop after getting off his shift. One evening, when he came home after the boys were already in bed, Mary was waiting for him with his dinner ready. She sat down with a cup of tea and smiled at him as he wolfed down his meal. "James, I have a surprise for you. We're going to have another baby in April. Maybe it will be a girl this time," she said hopefully.

James reached across the table and squeezed her hand. Joy was written all over his face. "Well," he whispered, "I guess I better learn to make girl toys too."

"Better wait and see," Mary laughed. "You'll have time to learn that next year."

"You're right," James nodded. "I'd better be thinking about bigger things, like how soon I can get our new home started. This one is going to be pretty crowded come next April!"

Christmas was almost as spectacular as the year before, but this time there was a beautiful wreath for Harlow on the church door for Christmas Eve. Hannah was an admirable hostess and everyone had a marvelous time. Christmas Day was the usual fantastic occasion, with delectable foods and incomparable company. Hannah thanked everyone for their love and support through her loss of Harlow, and for their enduring love and companionship every day. Everyone counted their blessings for the year and enjoyed the day's camaraderie. There was even a fresh snow of several inches to compliment the occasion.

That winter was hard on Mary. Being pregnant and with two energetic boys, her time in Gage was difficult, to say the least. The house they lived in was small and very confining, especially when it was too cold for the boys to go outside. There was little snowfall in Gage, so they wanted to go to Grandma

Hannah's where there was frequently enough snow to build snowmen and play in. Mary had to become very creative with games and activities to keep the boys busy. James could see it was wearing her down, but after February he felt it was too risky to travel back and forth to Silver City. He would take the boys to the workshop at the mine sometimes, just to give Mary time to relax and get some badly needed rest.

On the twentieth of April in 1886, Mary gave birth to George. She was a little disappointed as she was hoping for a girl this time. James leaned down and kissed her and whispered in her ear, "Maybe next time, but right now I think you've done a fine job giving me these three sons. I couldn't be more proud!"

Hannah was thrilled to have another grandson. "I know you're a little disappointed, Mary," she said. "But you've brought us these fine boys to carry on the Quigley name and that is a wonderful gift. George is a lucky boy to have such fine big brothers to teach him about the world they live in."

Chapter 14

Shortly after George's birth, James received a letter from Hannah telling him that Mary Louise was finally going to leave Silver City for New York. She was determined to be a performer, singing and dancing her way across the stage in the big city, and there was no stopping her.

One day while she was playing and singing at the saloon, a man from New York, who had just arrived on the El Paso stage, stopped in for a cold drink. Mary sang a song and did some dancing and the man was intrigued. He simply had to find out more about this beautiful young lady who could charm the skin off a snake.

Joe told him he would have to talk to Hannah, the saloon owner. He found her in the cafe and introduced himself as Bernard Trible. He told Hannah that he was passing through and had seen Mary Louise in the Saloon. "I know talent when I see it," he said convincingly. "This young lady is being wasted here in Silver City. I would like to represent her in New York.

I know people who can help refine her talents and give her a real shot at a performing career." He gave Hannah his card, which said he was with the New York City Theatre Company.

Hannah introduced Mr. Trible to Mary Louise and escorted them to a table in the corner of the saloon. He told Mary Louise that he was associated with a reputable theater in New York and could place people like her in positions where they could learn from well-known performers.

"If you work hard you will be on stage in no time," he told her smiling. "You are a natural, my dear young lady. You already have a stage presence and your voice is clear and concise. I'm certain learning dance routines won't be a problem for you. Who has taught you up to now?"

"Rose," Mary Louise replied nodding toward the Silver City Theater's location. She told Mr. Trible about how Rose had taken her under her direction and helped her learn to dance and read music.

"Would you be interested in coming to New York and trying out for my theatre company?" Mr. Trible asked.

"Oh!Yes!" she repied with a grin as big as Texas. "I most certainly would, uh, if my mother will allow it." She turned her sweet smile on Hannah.

"As if a Brahma bull could stop you" Hannah laughed. "We need to talk further, Mr. Trible. Come into the cafe for supper this evening and we'll continue this conversation."

"Me too?" Mary Louise asked with raised eyebrows.

"Yes, of course you too." Hannah smiled putting her arm around Mary Louise's shoulders. "You must know, Mr. Trible, this young lady is no mere fly-by-night. She is my daughter and I will stand for no foolishness. This is business and will be done in a business-like manner. I will be checking your references to be sure you are who you say you are."

Mr. Trible sensed that he had stumbled upon a rare gem in Mary Louise, and he was more than compliant with Hannah to see that all was above reproach. Mary Louise was ecstatic. She excused herself, then burst out the back door and ran the entire distance to the theater.

"Rose! Rose! Where are you," she shouted breathlessly.

"What?" Rose asked as

she emerged from her dressing room with a panic-stricken look on her face. "What's the matter, child?"

"Oh Rose, you'll never guess what just happened!" Mary Louise hugged her then began dancing around. "I'm going! I'm going to New York, Rose!"

"Mary, slow down and breathe. Tell me what is going on!" Rose demanded gently.

She told Rose what had just taken place at the saloon. Rose's eyes were wide with surprise.

"Trible? Bernard Trible?" she said in amazement. "I can't believe it! I've heard quite a bit about him and his agency. They have put some wonderful performers on the stages of New York and Boston. You are a very fortunate girl, Mary Louise!"

"He wants me to go try out for his theater. Rose you have to go with me!" Mary Louise said hugging Rose again. "After all, you've been my teacher, my inspiration. You simply *must* come, please, please?"

Mary Louise and Rose were on the train to New York two weeks later. Mary Louise was so excited she couldn't sleep. She asked Rose a thousand questions, some of them more than twice! Rose was extremely happy for her "pupil", as she referred to Mary Louise. "I've never brought any of the girls I've helped to New York. I am so happy to be able to do this with you, but you must dedicate yourself to doing whatever they say, Mary Louise. You must work hard. No, you must knock yourself out!" Rose coached her.

"Go beyond what they expect. Give them twice their money's worth! That's the

kind of gal I want to see.
Show them you are more than
a beginner. You've got
experience, even if it was in a
saloon in Silver City. They
don't know that, only Mr.
Trible does. Perform so well
they think you have been in
St. Louis or Chicago! Knock
'em dead!"

"I will, Rose. I won't let
you down. I won't let me down
either! This is what I truly
want and I will do everything
possible to be a success!"
Mary Louise said squeezing
Rose's hand.

"I know you will, Mary
Louise," Rose smiled patting
her hand. "I know you will."

Chapter 15

Mary Louise couldn't believe her eyes when she saw New York. She had never seen a city, so the size of New York, with so many people, was simply overwhelming. And just as Rose had told her, buggies were everywhere. Carriages and horse-drawn trolleys choked the streets, and an occasional steam-driven trolley would pass them, chugging along.

Mary Louise's eyes almost popped out of their sockets at the sight. She just looked at Rose and pointed in utter dismay. Rose nodded with raised eyebrows and took her arm as they strolled along the busy sidewalk, gazing into store windows and smelling the veritable banquet of aromas from all the different eateries. The buildings were so tall Mary Louise felt as though she were in a canyon. She almost tripped and fell trying to see the tops of them. The immensity of it all simply took her breath away. So many stores with so many different things; some with just hats, or just shoes, and some with just candy, not at all like the general store she was used to seeing. She shook her head and rolled her eyes in utter amazement.

"Oh, Rose!! This is better than I ever dreamed it would be!" Mary Louise said breathlessly. It was quite overwhelming to a young girl who had known nothing but small towns in mining and cattle country. After their brief glimpse of the city, they hailed a taxi buggy to take them to the theater where they were to call on Mr. Trible. The secretary said he was in a meeting.

When he learned Mary Louise and Rose were waiting, he excused himself so that he might welcome them. "Come ladies," he invited. "Let me show you around."

They went down the stairs to the second floor. "These areas are used for training, such as dance, voice and music lessons," he told them. Also, there were studios where scenery and stage props were designed and constructed.

The theater occupied the main floor with its grand decor and hundreds of seats. The stage was enormous compared to what Mary Louise had known in Silver City, where the dressing rooms had been like closets. Here the dressing rooms were large as a parlor with plenty of light, a mirror from ceiling to floor, and places to hang hats, clothes, even shoes.

Returning to the third floor, he explained these were offices for the people who ran the theater. Mr. Trible's office was cheery and had a spectacular view of Madison Avenue. He offered them beverages and asked if they would wait a few minutes while he finished some business.

"I have died and gone to Heaven, Rose!" Mary Louise whispered when they were finally alone. "I just can't believe I'm here and this is finally happening to me!"

Rose just smiled and nodded, knowingly, recalling her first time in New York. It was magical, mystical, and overwhelming to her then, just as it was to Mary Louise now. She had been twenty-three then and in love with the theater just as this young girl was. All would have been so wonderful, if it hadn't been for a man who charmed her and won her heart, then broke it.

Remembering Lou still would send a pang of hurt and anger through her. After that, she found it impossible to trust any man again. She had taken lovers on occasion, but never gave her heart away to any of them. Once was enough, she reassured herself, and resolved to keep the score as it was.

"This is our dance instructor, Willie McCaren," Mr. Trible said as he came through the door, startling both women out of their own private thoughts. "He will begin your training tomorrow, and when he feels you are ready he will put you in the chorus line. He will be your dance coach for as long as you remain, which will, of course, be determined by your progress," Mr. Trible smiled encouragingly.

Willie was a small, attractive man in his late thirties, with a lithe and easy manner about him. He smiled broadly as he shook Mary Louise's hand, and Rose's when Mr. Trible explained that she had been the girl's instructor for music and dance in New Mexico. He didn't say Silver City. It wasn't important to him where she had begun.

His interest was in seeing how well she could develop into a real performer. A fair chance was what he offered, nothing more, nothing less. He made that clear in a gentle, yet unquestionable manner.

"We'll get your dance togs together tomorrow before we begin class," Willie told Mary Louise in his light Irish brogue. "Eat a light breakfast and be ready to work," he said turning to leave. Then with a pat on her shoulder he said smiling, "We do have some fun when we work, too. Don't you worry," he winked at Rose. "She'll do just grand!"

"There is a small flat for you and Rose to live in," Mr. Trible told them when Willie had gone. "I'm sure you will find it comfortable and conveniently close to the theater. It's just around the corner past the tailor shop, then upstairs. I'd like to have you join me for dinner this evening. I've already made a reservation at Cecil's for seven. There's plenty of time for you to freshen up and rest. I hope that meets with your satisfaction," he smiled.

"Oh, yes, thank you!" Mary Louise replied with controlled enthusiasm. "Where shall we meet you?"

"I'll be at the entry door to your stairs at six thirty with a carriage waiting. I hope you brought your appetite with you," he smiled.

"She never travels without it!" Rose declared with a grin.

At six thirty two beautiful ladies came down the stairs to the waiting carriage. Mr. Trible nodded and smiled his approval. They looked fresh and radiant, belying the fact that they were both tired from the trip and all the excitement of the day. It was a most memorable evening of exceptional food and conversation. Bernard

Trible told one story after another about performers and performances in the theater.

The one thing he didn't do, to Rose's satisfaction, was probe either of them for their background information. Taking them at face value showed he was a fair and scrupulous man, and in so doing he had earned their respect and admiration.

"Get a good night's rest and I'll see you at seven in the morning in my office, both of you," Mr. Trible told them, with an ever-so-slight glance at Rose to confirm. Once upstairs in their flat, Mary Louise fell exhausted into bed with stars in her eyes. Sleep came quickly and dreams in multitudes.

A week had passed and Mary Louise was working hard to get the dance steps right. She had never had real dance lessons before, only what Rose had shown her. She was a fast learner and quickly memorized the chorus routine.

The show was to open in just six more weeks, so not a minute was spared.

She had made several new friends in the chorus line and was loving every day of her new life. She wrote to James and Mary often to tell them everything that she was doing and all about New York.

James had been up to Silver City to see how Hannah was getting along. "James, Mary Louise sent you a letter," Hannah said as she poured him another cup of coffee. "She is very busy getting ready for her first show, which opens in two weeks. Rose says she is doing remarkably well with the dance routines. They are having the time of their lives!"

"I'll pick up the letter in Cow Springs on my way home," James replied reaching for a piece of Nora's apple strudel Hannah had brought him. "I will sure be glad when they get the mail coming into Gage. Someone from the mine usually rides up and brings it back about every other day."

It was the twenty eighth of June, a clear, warm day coming on, when James left Hannah's to return to Gage. "You take care of yourself, Mother," James told her, giving her a big hug on the front porch.

"I will," Hannah smiled. "And you be careful too, James. I love you. Give Mary and the children my love." She stood on the porch waving as he drove off toward Cow Springs, his wagon kicking dust clouds into the early morning air.

James drove into Cow Springs a little after high noon. Hot and thirsty, he left the wagon in front of the blacksmith shop and walked over to the small shack that served as a saloon where a few ranch hands and miners were having a poker game. It looked as though they had been at it a while already.

"James!" Walt Andrews called out, motioning to him. "Barkeep, bring us another bottle!" Pulling out an empty keg for a stool, James sat down to be quickly dealt in. As the afternoon wore on, James was downing considerable amounts of whiskey, as were the others at the table.

A few had cashed in their chips and gone, while a handful of die-hards stayed on. When they would finish a bottle, James would throw it up in the air; draw his gun and fire, hitting the bottle every time.

It was almost sundown when the door swung open and another cowboy walked in. James turned in his seat, and to his utter dismay, saw John Dodson standing in the dusky light. This was the man who had taken him in a game back in eighty. A dark look fell across his face as his eyes focused intently on the man.

"Hey, John!" one of the men called to him. "C'mon over. We'll deal ya in!"

James stood up, wavering slightly and knocking his stool over. "Yeah, let this bastard join the game," he sneered. "He's a lousy cheat so you better watch him real close!"

The room suddenly got very quiet as James stood with his hand on his holster glaring at Dodson. He felt a rage surging through his every vein. His head was spinning from the whiskey, but he clearly remembered the night John Dodson cheated him out of a five hundred dollar poker pot.

One of the men tried to push James back down onto the empty keg stool, but when he fought back the men stepped away from him saying it was time to head out for some grub. James refused to leave and the air was thick with tension.

The barkeeper had his shotgun out and told the men to break up the game and get out before someone got hurt. Everyone cleared out, urging James along with them. Jed and some of the others mounted their horses telling James they were camped to the south of town if he wanted to come out and have some grub.

When the men were gone only a cloud of dust was left to settle. James stood alone outside the shack for a few moments, then staggered across to his wagon in the fading light. A minute or two later gunshots rang out shattering the stillness of Cow Springs.

Following the sound of gunfire, the barkeeper came out of the saloon and saw the Cow Springs ranch foreman, Chad, kneeling beside the body of a man lying beside the buckboard.

No one knows for sure what happened that evening after the men left the saloon. James Quigley was lying dead in a pool of blood with his gun still cocked to fire, but no one saw what had happened. The sheriff was beckoned and the barkeeper told him what had transpired in the saloon that afternoon. He sent a deputy to try to find John Dodson.

No one else had given much thought to the gunfire, because James had been shooting bottles in the saloon during the poker game. Now someone needed to answer to what had occurred that hot, dusty evening in Cow Springs.

Chapter 16

Mary was awake all night, restless and worried. James was usually home by dark. The only stop he would be likely to make was to rest his horse a bit. Every nerve in her body was sounding emotional alarms. Late the next morning, R. H. Speed knocked at her door. At the rail stood James' horse and wagon. Mary opened the door and paled at the sight of the wagon without James.

"Where's James? What's happened to him?" she managed as she grasped the doorway for balance.

"Mary," R.H. said, taking her arm to support to her as he ushered her back into the house. "I'm sorry to be bringing bad news."

"What is it?" Mary asked again, her voice faint and shaky.

"There was a shooting up

at Cow Springs," R.H. told her gently as he could. "No one knows what happened. Your husband was shot yesterday evening, ma'am. I'm real sorry. I need you to come up there. They are having the funeral today. I'd be happy to drive you there if you like. I know this is a terrible shock, ma'am. I am so sorry for you and the children."

Mary collapsed into a chair while R.H. brought her a glass of cold water. The shock was so great she couldn't even shed a tear. She just looked at R.H. as if she didn't know who he was or what he had just told her. It was a long few minutes before she could respond.

"1-1'll get the children ready," she said rising stiffly from her chair. R.H. offered to help and went to get Jimmy from the back yard while Mary rounded up George and Charlie.

Mary still had a glazed

look in her eyes as R.H. helped her and the boys into the wagon and drove them toward Cow Springs. It was a long, quiet ride and as young as they were, the boys seemed to know something was terribly wrong.

In Silver City, Sheriff Ray called on Hannah to tell her what had happened to James. Hannah just stared at him in disbelief.

"What are you telling me?" she asked him. "He just left here yesterday morning and he was fine," she said as the tears came into her eyes.

"Hannah do you remember John Dodson?" the sheriff asked her gently.

"Ye-yes," she stammered. "He and James had a falling out a few years back, over a poker game, if I recall correctly. But what's that got to do with anything?"

Sheriff Ray put his arm across her shoulder as he felt

her strength ebbing, and led her to a chair. "Yesterday afternoon James stopped at Cow Springs. He met up with some friends and played a little poker. They'd had quite a bit of whiskey, then Dodson stopped in and he and James had words.

"Dodson claims James shot first. He came in this morning to give himself up. There'll be a trial in two weeks. He'll be held in jail till then."

For Hannah it was the longest ride she had ever taken. She and James had always been very close. She couldn't imagine not having him in her life now. Her heart ached beyond comprehension.

Mary and the boys arrived at Cow Springs about the same time as Hannah and Sheriff Ray. The funeral was simple and brief, with only a few of the men from the ranch and a handful of miners there. After James was placed in the ground, Mary, Hannah, and the children stood at the site, the wind blowing as the sun sank low in the western sky.

"Mary," Hannah said taking Mary's arm in hers. "I would like for you and the children to come back and stay with me in Silver City. R. H. can have someone pack your things and bring them from Gage in a few days." Mary numbly nodded her assent as they walked toward where Sheriff Ray was waiting.

Hannah gave R.H. instructions and he reassured Mary that all would be attended to and for her not to be concerned. "Thank you, R.H.," Mary said, struggling to smile. "I appreciate all you've done." Then ushering her boys along, they got into the buggy with Hannah and headed for Silver City with Sheriff Ray following.

On July 2, 1886, this article was published in the

Cow Springs Shooting

A shooting occurred at Cow Springs on Monday evening last, in which James Quigley was killed by John Dodson, who the next morning came into the city and gave himself up. At the preliminary examination before Judge Givens on Wednesday afternoon all the evidence went to show that Quigley had been drinking heavily, and that in going home from Whitewater he went via Cow Springs several miles out of his way, evidently for the purpose of

217

"getting even" as
he expressed it,
with John Dodson,
whom he claimed
had done him
"dirt". After
arriving at the
springs he insisted
upon everyone
drinking, and after
they had a drink
he threw the empty
bottle into the air
and shot at it with
his pistol. Some of
the other boys at
the ranch, fearing
that there would
be trouble between
Quigley and
Dodson, tried to
get the former to
start home, but he
declined to do so.
Along toward
evening the boys,
for one reason or
another left the
house, leaving
Quigley and
Dodson alone.
Soon after their

leaving, the shooting began, three shots being fired. Dodson claimed that Quigley fired two shots before he could get his gun out. They were so close together when the first shot was fired that Dodson knocked Quigley's pistol up with his left hand, and then he jumped through a door into the house. Just as he entered the door Quigley fired again, the ball striking the casing of the door. Dodson then turned and fired going on into the room without stopping to see the effect of his shot. Quigley turned and walked a few steps towards his wagon and fell, dying in a few moments. He still held his cocked pistol in his hand. After the evidence was all in, Judge Givens discharged the prisoner, as it was shown beyond any doubt that the killing was done in self-defense. Quigley leaves a wife and three small children, and also a mother who runs a restaurant. The wife was brought over to the scene of the killing by R.H. Speed to attend the funeral. Quigley is said to have been a very desperate and bad man when under the influence of liquor, and it's claimed by parties

who knew him in Texas that he had killed five or six men previous to coming to this county. Dodson is a quiet, inoffensive, hardworking boy, and commands the respect of all who know him.

Hannah couldn't believe her eyes when she read the article. She'd had a run-in with Tom Ingles, the editor of the paper, about previous articles he had written saying she was a lady of the night and her saloon drew nothing but men of questionable character and means.

Tom also had written comments regarding her daughter, Mary Louise, implying she was a tramp who had run off to New York in search of a career in show business. Hannah wasn't going to let Tom get away with trash like that, and a few days after the article had printed, she went to confront him.

"Now Mrs. Walsh, I know you are upset, and if you want to make a statement I'll be glad to put it in the paper," he told her after some deliberation.

Hannah's statement read as follows:

> **Mrs. Walsh, of Central City (suburb of Silver City), mother of James Quigley, who was shot at Cow Springs nearly a month ago, called at this office last Friday. She desired to correct the impression created by the published accounts of her son's death, to the effect that he was a desperado or a "bad man"**

generally. She stated that he was a hard working and honest man who always took care of his family and treated everyone right.

He had, according to Mrs. Walsh's testimony, never killed but two men, and those he killed in self-defense in the state of Texas. The first one was trying to break into his house for the purpose of robbery, and the second was killed when advancing upon him with a dirk to stab him. Mrs. Walsh further desired it known that her son was at Cow Springs for the purpose of getting

**a letter he was
told was there for
him, and did not
go to provoke or
engage in any
quarrel.**
James was only twenty-seven
years old at the time of his
unfortunate death.

Chapter 17

Two years had passed since James' death. His sons were growing fast and had adjusted well considering all that had taken place in their young lives. Mary and Hannah had drawn strength and comfort from one another as they learned to accept their loss and go on with their lives.

It deeply saddened Mary that James would miss seeing his sons growing up. She would often tell the boys stories about their father so they wouldn't completely forget him. "He's always watching over you," she would reassure them often.

Sometimes she felt she would not survive the burden of sadness she bore, but Hannah's inner strength gave her courage, and she resolved to be the best mother she possibly could. James couldn't have asked for more, and

Hannah didn't.

In July the weather was hot and dry, as it had been for most of the summer. Everyone in Silver City was looking forward to the Fourth of July picnic, which was always the high point of the summer. Mary Louise was coming home for a visit, her first since James' death.

That had been a difficult time and she was very reclusive while with her family. She stayed only a few days, then had to return to the busy schedule to which she had committed in New York.

The excitement was mounting at Hannah's house at the approach of Mary Louise's arrival. Aunt Nettie and Nora could talk of nothing else and were cooking & baking up a storm in preparation for her visit. Mary's boys would hardly remember her, except for Jimmy, who thought the sun rose and set just for her. He told everyone about his

Aunt Mary Louise, the Broadway star. Mary Louise's letters to Hannah had indicated that Mr. Trible was extremely pleased with her progress, and had already billed her in his upcoming show, which would be performed in New York and Boston.

After months of voice, dance, and acting lessons, Mr. Trible was convinced beyond any doubt that Mary Louise's talent would be rewarded. She had become a well-heeled, beautiful young woman at the age of eighteen, and was well on her way to a successful career in show business.

Hannah had arranged for Mary Louise to perform for the Fourth of July picnic and a stage was erected at the end of Main Street for the evening festivities. A local band had been practicing music she had sent them in preparation for her town debut as a real Broadway performer. It was the talk of Silver City.

The Fourth dawned sunny, warm, and promising more heat as it wore on. There were streamers and banners in red, white and blue across the front of every building on Main Street and on the stage where the evening ceremonies would be held. Children were everywhere, helping their mothers take food to the picnic area, playing, shouting and running about in unbridled excitement.

Silver City was in a flurry of activity as the morning became afternoon and the picnic got underway. Folks from all over the area came into town to visit and enjoy the day's festivities.

Finally, as the shadows began to lengthen, a drum roll was heard from the ceremony platform and people began to pack their picnic goods and seek out a good place to sit or stand for the evening's event. The band struck up "I'm A Yankee Doodle Dandy" and everyone joined in the song. After Deacon Simmons offered a prayer and the mayor gave a short speech, Mary Louise was introduced.

She didn't disappoint the good folk of Silver City. They were entranced and amazed at how this young local girl could have become so captivating.

Tom, from the newspaper, even gave her a great write-up in his paper. He had also apologized to Hannah that afternoon about the article he had written in the paper about the Cow Springs shooting, which made James look like a "bad man."

Ironically, it was later learned that John Dodson was shot and killed in a poker game, somewhere in Colorado called Blackhawk, for trying to cheat in a card game. It seemed Fate had finally caught up with him.

Following the ceremony and Mary Louise's

performance, a dance began with the band playing favorite tunes along with a few new numbers. Mary Louise had brought some music from New York and they were delighted to introduce the new tunes. Everyone was having a wonderful time. Even the children were dancing.

Mary Louise danced with Jimmy, whose eyes sparkled with pure enchantment. He could speak of nothing else for days afterward. Hannah and Mary left to put George and Charlie to bed, then returned to enjoy the music. Mary noticed Aunt Nettie visiting with a handsome man she hadn't seen before.

As if reading her mind, Aunt Nettie began to walk in her direction with the fellow in tow. "Mary," she said smiling brightly, "I want you to meet John Stone. He's visiting some friends here in Silver City and said he would like to meet you. He is from the Oregon Territory in the far northwest, where Lewis and Clark came through when they found a way to the Pacific Ocean. There seemed a wee glint of cunning in Aunt Netties' eyes.

"Hello", Mary said softly, blushing as she shook his hand. "Would you care to dance?" he asked as the band began a waltz. "Yes, thank you," she smiled as he led her into the swirling throng.

John was in his early forties with dark hair showing some silver. He had intense dark brown eyes and a slightly crooked smile that gave the impression of constant humor. As they danced he asked her questions about Silver City and the surrounding area. He brought Mary back and asked Hannah to dance after Mary introduced them. Mary was intrigued with him from the start.

"Aunt Nettie," she said, "John seems very nice. How

do you know him?"

"Well, he came into the cafe a couple of weeks ago and we got to talking," Aunt Nettie told her. "He seems like such a fine man. He has been working with the Indian tribes up in the Northwest as a translator for the government. Perhaps he just wanted to visit the Southwest and meet some folks. I got the impression he wanted to meet a lady so, of course, I thought of you. I told him a little about you, and about the boys. Then I invited him to the Fourth of July festivities and he said he would come in the evening. He is nice, isn't he?"

"Aunt Nettie!" Mary exclaimed. "You're playing cupid! And, yes, he does seem very nice, but, well, I just feel so strange dancing with another man."

"Mary," Aunt Nettie smiled putting her arm around Mary's waist. "It's time you let go of the sorrow and live again. Perhaps John is just what you need, whether he stays around or not. You're still young and pretty, and you have three boys to raise. Just give it a chance and see what happens."

John and Hannah were laughing gaily as they came back to Mary and Aunt Nettie. "Your mother is most entertaining," he said to Mary. "I can see why folks love to come to her cafe and saloon. And of course, with Nettie's cooking who could refuse such hospitality! Now, if I may persuade you to dance with me again, Mary," he said taking her hand.

The evening flew by and Mary was learning about John and the work he did among the Indian people in the Northwest Territory. She could understand how those people would be drawn to trust him.

He spoke with such feeling in his voice and his

eyes reflected his sincerity when he talked about their problems and way of life. He was undoubtedly a very caring and understanding man. He told her much about the Northwest, and it was evident that he intended to return there after his visit in New Mexico.

John walked Mary home after the dance had ended, and asked if he could see her again in a week. Of course, she agreed.

"I have some business to attend to, but I shall come by as soon as I'm able," he told her. As he turned to go he squeezed her hand. "I shall not forget this evening and the lovely lady I've met. Thank you, Mary, for dancing with me."

That night Mary dreamed of tall redwood trees and fern-covered forest floors, and of a tall, handsome man with broad shoulders and warm brown eyes. John had made a profound impression on her and, although she chided herself for seeming too eager, she couldn't get him out of her mind.

During the days following their encounter, she found herself daydreaming about a place she had only seen through his eyes and words. What could it be like in such a place, she wondered. It was like a fairytale and, as the days passed, John became surreal, as well. On Saturday a letter came for Mary from Las Cruces, New Mexico.

John Stone had kept his word, and the letter said he would be in Silver City on Wednesday. Mary was elated. She shared the news with Hannah, who was also captivated with John's charming personality, as was Aunt Nettie.

Even Nora got to read the letter and smiled her approval. "It's time, my dear," she told Mary as they put another batch of strudel into the oven. "Nettie was very impressed with Mr. Stone. She told me she thought you would like him, and obviously you do!"

Mary blushed as their eyes met and they laughed knowingly. "He has captured my interest, I admit," she told Nora. "I hope he likes children, very lively children!" she grinned.

"I have a good feeling about him," Nora nodded. "From what Nettie said, and your mother's impression of him, I'd say he stands a good chance of becoming a regular visitor here."

"We'll see," Mary smiled. "I guess you're right, if even for the boys' sakes, it is time to go on with our lives. They need a father and there has been an undeniable emptiness in our lives without James. I just hope Hannah understands. I will always love James, you know."

"Of course she understands," Nora reassured her. "She understands a family needs a mother and a father. Hannah would never resent having a good man come into your life.   She's a wise and loving woman. Have no fear, Mary. She only wants the best for you and her grandchildren."

Chapter 18

John Stone came to Silver City as planned, and after locating a rooming house, went directly to Hannah's cafe. "Mrs. Walsh," he greeted Hannah when she came in from the saloon to welcome him. "I hope you don't mind if I see Mary. I understand the situation and would ask your approval before any further encounters with your daughter-in-law. I hope you have no misgivings about me seeing her."

"Mr. Stone," Hannah replied trying to sound stern. "You may see her only under these conditions."

John stepped back a little surprised at her response.

"You must treat her kindly and her sons as well. If you break her heart I will never forgive you. Mary is very precious to me, and so are my grandsons. I just ask that you understand that," Hannah told him smiling and patting his shoulder.

"Whew!" John said relieved. "I'm certainly glad you feel that way. I'd not want to do anything to cause further pain to any of your family. I assure you, Mrs. Walsh, my intentions are of the highest honor."

"Good," Hannah smiled. "I believe you will find Mary at home with the boys, and looking forward to your visit. Have a pleasant afternoon, Mr. Stone!"

With that, John kissed Hannah's hand and told her she was a fine lady indeed, and to please call him John. A few minutes later he approached Mary's front porch where three young faces peered out the window in unabashed curiosity. He waved at them laughing, his heart already stolen by their spirit.

Mary opened the door as all three youngsters peered at this tall stranger from behind her.

"I come bearing gifts," John told her as he brought a brown package from behind his back.

The moment he stepped into the house he felt the sense of acceptance and affection. He sat down and called the boys over after they had been introduced. "I've brought you some very unusual gifts," he said.

"My Shoshone friends sent them to you hoping you would like me and accept me as your guest."

The boys were glued to his side, even though George wasn't really old enough yet to understand all that was going on. From the package John pulled a beaded shirt made of doeskin. He held it up to Jimmy, whose eyes were the size of walnuts. "I think this will fit perfectly," John nodded to him smiling.

"Take it and try it on, Jimmy." Then he took out a leather thong with beads and a bear claw on it. "This is for protection from danger, Charlie. How do you like it?"

Charlie was in awe as John slipped the necklace over his little head. He smiled up at the man and, at Mary's prodding, said, "Tank oo.. Misser S'one."

For George, he had brought a pair of tot-size beaded moccasins. "And for you, Mary," John said smiling with his lips and eyes, "here's something for you, too." He handed her a three-strand necklace made of shell and beads, with hand carved fetishes.

It was a beautiful gift and Mary was astonished at the thoughtfulness of this kind and generous man and his friends. "John, these are wonderful gifts. Please thank your Shoshone friends, and tell me more about them," Mary said as she put George's little moccasins on his feet.

"I'll tell you anything you wish to know, Mary. One thing that is special about the Shoshone, they cherish their children," John said with a tender look toward George. "And speaking of that, I'd like to take you and the boys to meet them some day.

They are such interesting people and very curious about the white way of life."

They spent the rest of the afternoon visiting and enjoying the camaraderie of the boys. George sat on John's lap playing with the thong around his neck, which held a small leather bag. John explained to Jimmy, who inquired about it, that it was a medicine bag to fend off evil and give him strength and power.

At dinner he continued to fascinate them all with stories about life among the Shoshone people, and some time spent among the Nez Perce tribe in the Northwest.

"I wike da Norfest," Charlie grinned at John.

"You surely would, young man," John laughed. "It's a whole different world up there. You would learn much and grow tall and strong like the redwood trees."

Charlie laughed, nodding his head emphatically.....and everyone laughed at Charlie.

When Mary finally got the two younger boys to bed, she, John and Jimmy sat on the front porch and enjoyed the evening. Nora stopped by on her way home and asked Jimmy if he'd like to go home with her. It was a difficult decision until she declared that she had leftover strudel and no one to eat it. With that Jimmy was up in her wagon in a flash.

With the children out of sight John and Mary could finally be alone. The conversation eventually turned to her raising the boys without James, and about James, himself. "He was a good man, John," Mary told him frankly. "In spite of what some people thought after the newspaper article, he was a wonderful husband and devoted father.

"He was also an excellent shot, and I don't think he would have missed his target if he had shot first. But I wasn't there and no one saw what actually happened. I just think Mr. Dodson got what was coming to him up in Blackhawk. I've had a lot of help from Aunt Nettie, Nora, and, of course, Hannah. She's been like a mother to me and she adores these boys."

"I can see that," John smiled. "She's quite a lady and she thinks the world of you, Mary. I'm mighty glad I have met all you fine folks. My business in New Mexico and Arizona should be finished in about another month or so. I hope we can spend much of that time getting to know each other better.

"My friends, of course, have asked about you, since I'm not spending much time with them," he laughed. "I want to take you to their place and introduce you. How about Sunday evening?"

"I'd be honored, Mr. Stone," Mary replied smiling and feeling warm all over in his tender gaze.

For the remainder of that week Mary and John were together every day. John would come by and play with the boys, taking them on walks and teaching them much about the country they lived in. In the evenings he and Mary would go for long walks and occasionally a buggy ride, while he told her more about the Northwest Territory.

She was in awe when he said the redwood trees were so large that it took as many as ten men holding hands to circle one tree, and how beautiful the ocean was. When he described the rivers and salmon runs, and told her how often it rained, she just shook her head in dismay.

She had never seen the ocean, much less all that much rain! She had been living in the desert most of her life, where rain fell infrequently and there were few rivers that weren't dry most of the year. He told her about the beautiful flowers that bloom year round and how everything stayed green all year as she stared off into the distance trying to imagine such a place.

John was scheduled to

leave New Mexico the end of December to travel to Santa **Fe.** Trying not to show her sadness, Mary felt a sense of dread as the time drew near. "I'll be back in three weeks, Mary, so don't you worry," John told her reassuringly.

"I wouldn't even be leaving if it weren't a very important trip. There is so much we need to talk about when I return, so please wait for me. I'll think of you constantly while I'm away. I love you, Mary. I hope you won't take another suitor before I return."

"I'll try to fend them all off at the door!" Mary laughed. Then she experienced the most romantic farewell kiss of her life. As he walked away she hoped he would come back, to stay in her life forever.

Chapter 19

John arrived back in Silver City three weeks later and Mary was jubilant. She didn't think she would be capable of loving anyone again. After all, she and James had known each other for a long time and were certain they would always be together. Since being widowed she had given little thought to meeting another man or to marriage.

John was different from James in many ways. He was soft-spoken, gentle, and more patient than any man she had ever met. Mary could understand why he had a job working with the Indian people. He showed such kindness and patience with the boys, and kept them intrigued with his stories of the Northwest Territory and the native people there.

When John came to see

her he presented her with a package telling her, "This is quite fragile, Mary. It's something very special just for you." When she unwrapped it she was astonished to behold a beautiful piece of pottery.

"Oh, John!" she exclaimed breathlessly. "This is so beautiful! Thank you so much!"

"I was in a Pueblo village and met a woman there who does exquisite pottery. She offered this to me saying it would be a fitting gift for you. I have some things for the boys, too," he smiled, as if knowing they were within earshot. In a moment's time they were at his side anxiously waiting to unwrap their gifts.

Beautifully decorated rattles and a drum were presented to them, and as the cacophony of the instruments prevailed, Mary frowned at

John. "So much for peace and quiet!" she declared. They both laughed as the boys began dancing around the room in Indian fashion demonstrating their talents.

That night, after the boys were put to bed, John built a fire in the fireplace and beckoned Mary to come join him. He picked up the pottery he had brought that afternoon, and placed it before her again. "What I didn't tell you earlier when I gave you this gift, Mary, is that this is called a wedding olla." It was then that John asked her to marry him. She was delighted, and accepted with an elated, "Yes!"

When they were told the news, the boys were thrilled to know that John was going to be their new father. They were all so young when James was killed that they hardly remembered him. They loved John and often affectionately referred to him as "uncle". He was very obviously fond of them too, and so ensued a strong bond of affection which lasted throughout their lifetimes.

On the twenty-fourth of February in 1889, John and Mary were married before a gathering of friends and family. They made a handsome couple. John, with his rugged good looks, dark hair and dark brown eyes made a fetching groom. Mary, so petite with her russet hair wrapped in flowers, and her dancing green eyes, was the envy of many a spinster that day. Rev. C. A. Laraway, Justice of Peace of Silver City, performed the ceremony. John's long-time friend Henry W. Long, and Mary's friend, Mary A. Laraway, stood up for them, along with Mary's three proud sons.

To everyone's delight, Mary Louise was there to sing for the newlywed couple at their reception at Pleasant

Valley, where Hannah, Aunt Nettie and Nora had outdone themselves for a gala celebration. Mary Louise's beauty, punctuated with her mastery of voice, was the topic of much conversation in Silver City for weeks afterward.

Rose had not come with her that trip, as she was planning her own wedding in New York to none other than Mr. Trible. The engagement had been the talk of the town until Mary Louise showed up. Everyone wanted to ask her about Rose and the wedding plans. The question arose a number of times about Mary Louise and a prospective husband, but she just smiled coyly and changed the subject with finesse.

Having arrived a few days prior to the wedding, she did spend some time with Hannah talking about her career and seeking her motherly advice in various personal matters. She also spent as much time as possible with Aunt Nettie, who had been a prominent support in her pursuit of a musical career.

Now there was the speculation as to what she would do after Rose was married. Surely Hannah and Aunt Nettie had an inside track on that information, but they weren't saying a thing.

Mary, too, was tight-lipped when prodded with questions from friends. Mary Louise was keeping her life private, if not a bit mysterious, to her hometown fans.

Two months after the wedding, Mary faced the sorrowful occasion of bidding farewell to Aunt Nettie, Nora and Hannah. She knew it would be a long time before she would see them again, if ever. She felt a mixture of sadness and excitement as she, John and the boys boarded the train bound for

San Francisco, California. The boys, Jimmy, age six; Charlie, age five; and George, age four, were all exhilarated about riding the train and spent hours during the trip gazing out the windows at the passing desert, mountains and canyons.

After they arrived in California, they would be boarding a ship bound for the Northwest Oregon Territory. It was going to be a long, arduous trip, and Mary made every effort to be strong and keep faith they would all arrive safely in Oregon.

John had told Mary about his cousin, Jeff, and his wife, Charlene, who lived in a small town by the name of Gold Beach, right on the ocean, and how much they loved it there.

The cousins were delighted to have John returning with his new bride and the boys, and stood ready to help them get settled in their new home. John sincerely hoped Mary would be content in the country he held in such great esteem.

Folks were coming to the Northwest by way of the ocean, while others were traveling by land over the plains, bringing whatever they could to start a new life in this promising new territory. There were abundant opportunities for the new settlers. Fishing was excellent, and there was rich soil where one could grow a hearty garden or a plethora of crops. Fruit trees grew easily and flowers bloomed the year round.

Pastures were green and lush and trees for timber were plentiful. It seemed the perfect environment for anyone willing to settle and get a new start. Mary was excited about all she had heard of the Oregon Territory, and the boys were wild with anticipation. They were looking forward to seeing the huge trees John had told them about, as well as the beautiful seacoast there.

It was a long trip on the train and the boys were restless the entire time, anxious to arrive and see the ocean for the first time. Mary had never seen the ocean either, and when she did she was amazed at the beautiful blue expanse of the Pacific. San Francisco offered its own variety of sights, being perched on hills overlooking the bay. John took them down to the docks to see if the ship Mary D. Hume was in.

He had taken voyage on the vessel up the coast before, and assured Mary it was going to be a safe trip. She was rather apprehensive since she was only accustomed to land travel by stage or train.

Picture of the Mary D Hume earlier as a whaling ship, and as she sits now in the Rogue River in Gold Beach Oregon

Mary D Hume

257

Chapter 20

The ship, the Mary D. Hume, had been built in 1880, on the Rogue River. It was ninety feet long, the largest single stick of square timber that ever floated down the Rogue River at that time. The ribs were handmade from Port Orford cedar roots dug from the ground before cutting. This was done to preserve the natural curvature of the roots, which were then fastened together by myrtle wood dowels, secured by locust wedges. She was built strong and sturdy for the fierce Pacific winter storms.

First used as a tugboat on the rough Pacific, this was to be the last voyage carrying passengers. The Mary D. Hume was being sold as a whaling ship, and was due to have a makeover on her next trip back to San Francisco. The ship operated between San Francisco, as the southern terminal, and Ellensburg (later named Gold Beach) on the Rogue River, traveling, as well, on the Siuslaw River, the Smith River to Coos Bay, and occasionally, Port Orford, which happened to be John and Mary's point of destination. However, they decided instead to disembark at Gold Beach, where John's cousin, Jeff, would be waiting to meet them.

Along with a few other passengers, there was also a large cargo of general supplies, including machinery, manufactured goods, and textiles. It was a trip Mary said she would never take again. Everyone was seasick the entire trip, which lasted a miserable ten days. They had encountered a storm at sea, and were tossed about until they all had bruises to show for it. When they were approaching the Rogue River, they saw a man on the beach waving a big sign telling them it was allright to come into the river entrance.

That was the only way

they had of knowing it was safe to enter the river. On one side of the sign it said "OK", in big letters, and on the other side it said, "NOT OK." Mary was never so happy in her whole life as when she walked off that ship onto firm, dry land.

Waiting for them on the dock were John's cousin Jeff, his wife, Charlene, and their two children. After the introductions, Jeff said, "We've got a place all ready for you. It's not much, but in a month or so, I figure we can all work together and build you a nice home where Mary will have a view of the ocean."

Mary didn't sleep well that night with the wind howling through the walls making strange sounds. John hugged her tight, knowing she the move to Oregon was a big adjustment for her. In spite of its overwhelming beauty it was still a rugged, and somewhat hostile country. Many of the Indians were basically uncivilized and a challenge to deal with in the most simple circumstances. There were those who did interact with the whites, but they were few.

The undergrowth was so thick you couldn't see five feet off the road for all the ferns and brush, but the trees and vistas were splendid. Clearing a plot would take considerable time and effort, but the logs would be put to good use after cutting. It was late April, and the flowers were in bloom everywhere she looked, in every color of the rainbow and then some. Mary had never seen anyplace so breathtakingly gorgeous.

Chapter 21

Throughout the entire summer John, his cousin, Jeff, and all the boys worked hard on clearing the land and building the house. It would be the nicest home she had ever known, other than Aunt Nettie's place in Kansas. It sat on a knoll overlooking the ocean at the edge of the town of Port Orford.

Mary couldn't wait to move in. Finally on the fifth of July in 1891, John came knocking on the door of their temporary home, and when Mary answered it, there he stood with a huge smile and a fist full of flowers. "Mary, my love, the house is finished. You may begin moving in any time."

With tears of joy she threw her arms around him, crying with delight. After a moment she told him, "I have a surprise for you too." Then with a coy smile she said,

"We are going to have a baby to help fill up the new home."

John just stood looking at Mary, disbelief spread across his rugged features. The impact of what she had just said brought a shout and laughter. A child of his own! It wasn't that he didn't love Jimmy, Charlie, and George, but a baby of his own was wonderful news. A new home and a new baby, this truly would be a wonderful life indeed!

They were moved in and settled in their new home by Christmas of that year, and it was a Christmas they would never forget. Mary set about to decorate in the manner of her mother, Hannah, in Silver City. She was intent upon sharing the holidays in a most festive way possible, and she was extremely successful. The boys were caught up in her determination and they virtually overwhelmed John in all they were able to do to make that first Christmas in Oregon one of lasting impression.

On the twenty first of January in 1892, their daughter, Ruth was brought into the world yelling and healthy. The boys were thrilled to finally have a little sister. Competition ran high as to which of them would be her greatest protector.

Two years later the miracle was repeated and Bessie was born on the first day of May in 1894. She, too, was welcomed with effusive love by her siblings. On the twenty second of September in 1896, a son was born and named after his father, John. It had been a blessed life in Oregon for Mary and John.

The family was growing and had prospered in their new home, and more people were continually moving to Oregon bringing school teachers, doctors, and merchants, adding much to their little community. The children had good schools and education was an important asset to that portion of the Northwestern frontier.

Jimmy, Mary's oldest son, was becoming quite a handsome young man. He still looked a lot like Mary, but had James' dark curly hair, blue eyes, and lithe, strong body. The girls at school would giggle and whisper when he walked by hoping he would smile at them. Several were vying for his attention, but he remained just warm and friendly.

He had gone to work for Jeff, who had bought a mill not far from Port Orford, about twelve miles north of Gold Beach. The mill produced cedar shingles, which turned out to be a solid and profitable business. There were more orders than could be filled, so Jimmy and Charlie, both worked late into the evenings on most days. Many nights they were so tired they would just go straight to bed without eating, much to Mary's chagrin. She was determined that they would all have good, hearty meals to keep them healthy and strong. Her garden attested to her intent, bursting with a bounty of vegetables from early summer to late autumn.

As the Fourth of July was approaching, plans were underway and the whole town had planned to get together for a large picnic at the beach. The year was 1901, and Jimmy, at eighteen years of age, was looking forward to getting a day off from work. Mary and the girls had been busy as bees the morning of the holiday baking pies, frying chicken, and making lemonade. It was going to be a fun day for the whole family.

Jeff and his family were coming, too. They now had seven youngsters to tend. Mary and Charlene had become good friends, helping each other with raising the children, working together as cooperative mothers and child caretakers.

It was a perfect day at the beach for the picnic. The wind was calm and everyone was having a wonderful time splashing in the water, playing games, and building sand castles, while eating as much as they could hold. After consuming more than his share, Jimmy decided to lie down on the blanket where he soon fell asleep. With a scream that shook Jimmy awake, a most attractive young girl fell right on top of him trying to catch a ball.

"Oh my, I'm so sorry," she laughed with no sign of true remorse. "My name is Jessie. What's yours?"

Jimmy, with his face full of sand, was trying to think straight, while Jessie was trying to brush the sand off him.

"Uh..ahh," he stuttered. "Jimmy," he finally managed. "My name is Jimmy."

Jessie plopped down next to him and looked straight into his questioning eyes and began to giggle. "I really am sorry. I hope I didn't startle you too much," she said

"It's okay," he replied. "I guess it was time I woke up anyway." His laugh was warm and genuine, and his eyes sparkled with curiosity. "I haven't seen you around here before," he told her. "You said your name was Jessie?"

"That's right," she replied smiling. "We live in Sixes, six miles north of here. Been there for about five years now. Want to come and meet my family?"

Jimmy got up slowly, still a bit off balance, and Jessie took his hand, to pull him up. They walked down the beach a short ways where her family was gathered.

"Mother, Daddy, this is Jimmy," she told them, adding, "I just ran into him on the beach." She looked at Jimmy and winked and they both began laughing.

"And these are my sisters Gussie and Roda. We came from Ohio. Where are you from?" she asked him.

"We came here from New Mexico," Jimmy told her. "Did you come along the Oregon Trail, Jimmy?" Jessie's mother, Ida, asked.

"No, ma'am," he replied. "We came up the coast on the ship Mary D. Hume from California."

"Say! I'd like to hear about that trip sometime," Jessie's father, Tom Cornwell, told him. "We came by way of the Oregon Trail."

"I'd surely like to hear about that!" exclaimed Jimmy. "That must have been quite an adventure!"

Jessie was seventeen years old, a pretty girl with dark long hair, expressive dark brown eyes, and full of fire. Jimmy thought she was about the cutest girl he had ever seen and they spent the next several hours laughing and talking while watching the younger children play on the beach. The sun was casting long beams of golden light across the water when Jessie's mother called for her to help pack up their things to leave.

"Jessie, can I see you again?" Jimmy said hopefully.

"I'd like that," she replied smiling brightly. "When you get to Sixes, go to the first road at the edge of town, then to the right, over the hill and down about a mile. It's a white house trimmed in green with a giant pine tree in the yard. You can't miss it."

"May I come see you next Sunday?" he ventured, uncertain of his feelings. This was foreign territory to Jimmy and he spoke with trepidation.

"Yes," Jessie replied, blushing. "That would be fine." Then, in a heartbeat, she whirled and was running down the beach. More like flying, actually. Her heart was light as a feather and she was sure she was flying.

Chapter 22

It was a few weeks after the Fourth of July when Mary got a letter from Aunt Nettie.

July 8, 1901

Dear Mary,

It has been a bad couple of weeks here. I have been down with some kind of cold, not a good thing in this hot weather. Nora has been so kind, caring for me. I just don't know what I would do without her. But she is getting old, too, and it's hard for her to do the work she has been doing these past years. She is only baking pies once a week now for the soldier's camp at

Fort Bayard. Mary Louise is doing fine for herself. She now has her own dancing and acting troupe and is in demand all over the country. Even some folks in England are asking her to perform there.

I'm sorry to have to tell you that our precious Hannah had a stroke last week, and passed away on the seventh of July. She was fifty-four years old. We will miss her terribly. It's a blessing that she didn't suffer, but died peacefully in her sleep. That is all for now please give the boys my love.

Love, Aunt Nettie

Mary was heartbroken about Hannah. She had truly been like a mother to Mary. She felt her world tilt in its orbit, such was the depth of her loss.

She dreaded telling the boys their Grandmother Walsh had died. It seemed so long ago when they had last seen her. She wished they would have been able to visit, at least so Hannah could have seen their other children and the wonderful home John had made for them in Oregon.

John shared her sorrow, and Jimmy, who clearly remembered his wonderful Grandmother, was extremely sad to know he would never see her again. It was the first time he had given any serious thought to death, and it moved him deeply. It took some time for Mary to fully recover and accept Hannah's death; her sorrow was enduring.

It was a fairytale summer for Jimmy and Jessie, though. Every day he could get away from work early, he would head for Sixes and the Cornwell house to see Jessie. They spent their time together having picnics, riding horses on the beach, and picking wildflowers for each other. It was readily apparent they were falling in love, and everyone knew it but them. Folks said they made a cute couple, both full of fire. "Oh, we're just friends!" they would say.

Lois Lewis was Jessie's best friend, and Jessie had no idea Lois had loving eyes for Jimmy. One day on the beach Jessie had to leave Jimmy's company early and Lois was standing on the hill just behind them hoping she could get Jimmy alone. This was her chance, so she waited until Jessie was out of sight, then she made her move. "Jimmy, is that you?" Lois said in her sweetest voice. "I saw Jessie had to leave. Did you two have a fight?"

"No, she just had some things to do at home," Jimmy replied completely unaware of Lois' intent.

"Will she be coming back?" Lois asked as she drew closer to where Jimmy was sitting.

"I don't think so," Jimmy said innocently.

Easing herself down onto the blanket, Lois said coyly, "May I sit here and talk to you for a while?"

"If you like," he replied nonchalantly. As she talked about the ocean and then about the beautiful day, she began to run her fingers through his curly hair and tickle him behind the ear.

Jimmy didn't quite know what to think about that. All he knew was that it felt kind of nice. Then Lois leaned over and kissed him. Jimmy took

the bait and kissed her back.
He felt the flames of passion
licking at him, but failed to
step aside.

The kissing continued
unabated and things started
getting out of hand. Abruptly,
Jimmy pulled free and caught
his breath. "Lois, I have to go
now!" he said jumping up. He
ran all the way to his horse,
jumped on, and didn't look
back. Lois stood there quite
flushed with a sly grin on her
face. Next time, she thought,
he won't be able to resist. I'll
let him have his way with me
and then Miss Jessie will lose
her sweetheart.

Mary handed Jimmy an
envelope when he came home
from the mill one evening
shortly after the beach
incident with Lois. It read:
Surprise
Birthday
Party For
Lois M.
Lewis,
who is

turning
18.
Please
come on
Saturday,
August
15th,
1901.
Cake and
ice cream
will be
served at
5:00 P.M.
sharp.

Jessie had a date with Jimmy that weekend. "Jimmy, we can go there together, although I'm sure Lois wants you to come alone. She likes you, you know," she smiled knowingly.

Jimmy thought about the brief encounter with Lois on the blanket at the beach, but had never said anything to Jessie. After some hesitation, he said, "Well, I guess we could go there for a while." Jessie didn't see the guilty look in his eyes as he turned them away. His heart was pounding with anxiety. If Jessie ever found out...

The day of the party they met at Jimmy's house then went together in a buggy to Jessie's place.

"Surprise!! Happy Birthday!!" everyone shouted when Lois came in the door. There were about ten of her friends that had come to regale her on this special occasion. After some party games and gifts, when everyone had eaten all the ice cream and cake they could hold, they started toward their homes, as evening was coming on. "Jimmy, will you come back after you take Jessie home?" Lois whispered to him as he went outside. "There's something I'd like to talk to you about."

"Well, o-okay, I guess," Jimmy stammered. "But I'll have to head on home myself real soon."

During the ride to Jessie's house, Jimmy was rather subdued, wondering what Lois wanted to talk to him about. Jessie seemed not to notice his quietness and talked as she usually did, about all sorts of things.

When he returned about an hour later, Lois met him at the door. "Come sit on the porch with me, Jimmy. I want to learn more about you. I feel like we have so much in common." Everyone was gone by that time, and it was nearly dark. Lois' folks had gone to do some chores for a neighbor who was laid up with a broken arm, she told him as he walked around to the porch.

Jimmy sat down on the porch swing where Lois invited him with a pat of her hand. She began asking him things about where he grew up and about his job. She told him how she admired him and then brazenly put her arms around his neck and kissed him passionately. Pressing her body into his she made every effort to turn him on. It didn't take long and quickly things got out of hand, and this time Jimmy couldn't stop. Next thing he knew they were lying on the porch under the swing without any clothes on.

"Oh no! Lois, I'm so sorry!" he said pulling on his pants. "I just got so carried away!"

Smiling, Lois took his chin in her hands and kissed him. "That was best birthday present I could have ever gotten, Jimmy Quigley."

When they were dressed again, Lois took his hand and followed him to the to the porch steps. "I've got to be going," he said with more gruffness in his voice than he intended.

"Farewell, my sweet," Lois murmured, as she waved to him. Oh Lordy, Jimmy thought to himself. Jessie would never understand how this could have happened. I never meant it to happen. He was a very perplexed and guilt-ridden young man when he left Lois' house that night.

The next couple of weeks, Jimmy avoided all contact with Lois, and hadn't seen much of Jessie, either. He was putting in more hours at work and going straight home every night. On Friday evening of the following week, when his family had gone into town for a social dinner, Jessie knocked on Jimmy's door, much to his surprise.

"Hey, Jessie," he said smiling with genuine delight when he saw her standing there.

When she looked up at him there were tears trickling down her cheeks. "Lois told me what happened, Jimmy," she said taking her eyes from his. "She bragged about how she got you to make love to her. I hate her! I want to kill her!" she hissed.

Jimmy took Jessie in his arms but she started to resist. He pulled her to him and held her for a few moments. Then he lifted her chin and kissed her tenderly. "Lois means nothing to me, Jessie. Please believe that. I don't even know how it happened, it just did, and I'm so sorry. I was ashamed to see you again. I knew if you found out you'd be hurt and I was afraid you would hate me, too," he told her softly.

"Oh, Jimmy, I do love you," she whispered, holding him closer. Jimmy kissed her again, then picked her up and carried her into the house. He laid her down gently on the bed and lay down beside her.

"Jessie, I love you too. Can you ever forgive me?" Again they kissed and then the passion consumed them both. Jimmy was ever so gentle so as not to frighten

Jessie. She had never dreamt making love could be so wonderful. Afterward they lay there for a long time not speaking, just holding each other close.

"Jessie, I love you, and I'll never let anything like what happened between Lois and I ever happen again," Jimmy promised. "Not ever!"

Right side of table James and Jesse their wedding reception
                                    April
2, 1902

Chapter 23

It was just a few weeks before Christmas and Jessie and Jimmy had just come in from putting the livestock in the barn. The weather was turning colder and storms were blowing in from the ocean, one right after the other. The house was cozy and warm with a big fire glowing in the fireplace. Jessie and Jimmy had spent many hours in front of that hearth talking and playing checkers or mending tack for the horses.

"Jimmy, why don't you plan on joining us for Christmas dinner this year?" Jessie's mother said as they sat down to Sunday evening dinner.

"I would surely love to," he replied. "I'll have to make apologies to my mother, though. She loves to have all our family together."

Christmas day was cold and windy as Jimmy hitched up the buggy and headed out for Jessie's house. He could smell the food before he got to the door. On the gaily-decorated table were roasted goose, fresh cranberry salad, butter rum cake, and apple and cherry pies like Nora used to bake. Memories of many past Christmases with his Grandma Hannah flooded his mind and tugged at his heartstrings. Yet this Christmas was to be the most special of all for him. He had a plan.

"Please come in Jimmy," Ida said before taking his coat. "It sounds like a bad storm is blowing in tonight. You may have to spend the night here, so put your horse and buggy in the barn, just in case."

They sat down to a sumptuous meal, and Jessie proudly told Jimmy she baked the pies and made the cranberry salad. Jimmy just

you knew what a stove was,
He just smiled.

Punching his shoulder in
fun, she said, "There's more
to me than you can imagine,
Mr. Quigley!"

After dinner, Jimmy
went into the sitting room and
asked Mr. Cornwell if he
might have a word in private.
"Sir," he began nervously, "I
would like to ask for your
daughter's hand in marriage. I
know we're young but I've got
a good job and feel we are
ready to break out on our
own."

Mr. Cornwell lit his
pipe, not saying a word.
Jimmy stood there not
knowing what to say or do.
After a few moments, Mr.
Cornwell looked at him
nodding. "So you want my
daughter's hand, do you? What
does she say about this?"

"Well, sir, I haven't
asked her yet, but I think she
will agree to it," Jimmy
replied confidently.

Suddenly Jimmy heard a

noise behind him and when he turned he saw Jessie standing there with a glowing smile on her lips. "Well, son, I guess there's your answer," Mr. Cornwell chuckled.

Jessie took Jimmy's hand and squeezed it tight. "You can ask me anytime now!" she said laughing as Jimmy put his arms around her and hugged her. Shaking Mr. Cornwell's hand, he said, "I'll take good care of her, sir. She's the best thing that's ever happened to me!"

On the second of April in 1902, Jimmy and Jessie were married. Gussie and Roda were bridesmaid and maid of honor, and Charlie was Jimmy's best man. The whole town turned out for the wedding—all, that is, except Lois, who, for some reason never received an invitation.

Both families helped the newlyweds get their home built that summer, a small place not far from their parents. They were given some livestock as wedding presents so they could get a herd of beef cattle started. Through John's friendship with the Nez Perce, Jimmy was able to get some fine horses for breeding. They had all they needed for a secure future.

Jimmy worked hard with his livestock and had some of the finest horseflesh in the county to sell. His studs were booked months ahead and many of the colts were being readied to show on the major circuits as soon as they were of age. Trainers and riders alike were greatly impressed with the speed and agility of the breed, which evolved and became known as the appaloosa.

On the fifth of February in 1904, a son was born to Jessie and Jimmy. They named him James Evert Quigley, keeping the tradition of Jimmy's family by naming the first son James. That same year Jimmy's brother, Charlie, moved away to California. Jimmy was sad to see him go, but knew Charlie had a mind of his own and had wanted to leave Oregon for some time. Oddly, Charlie never married.

Two years later, on the thirteenth of January in 1906, a daughter, Noma, was born to Jessie and Jimmy. The following year on December twenty-seventh, 1907, another son, Stanley, was born. About that same time Jimmy's youngest brother, George, courted and wed Sylvia Clarno. Together they had three children, Norman, Earl, and Wanda. George became one of the early stage drivers in Curry County.

Though Jimmy and Jessie truly felt love for one another, they were quite different personalities. Jessie was always full of energy and excitement, and having three babies seemed to take a lot out of her. Evert was six,

Noma was four, and Stanley was two years old when Jessie began to undergo noticeable change. She became quieter and distant, and her interest in the children was diminishing. She and Jim didn't talk much with each other, mostly just to the children, who were everywhere all the time. They took a great deal of time and energy from Jessie, and the wear was showing in her face. Bouts of depression set in and became more and more frequent. Sometimes she would just close the bedroom door and keep to herself for a whole day. It was obvious to Jimmy's family that the marriage had hit rocky ground.

One morning in late July, Jim injured his knee while pulling green lumber off the belt at the Port Orford Mill, so he left early in the afternoon and headed home. When he arrived he saw Sam Wester's horse tied up out back of the house. Very quietly he went into the house and down the small hallway where he heard moaning. With jaws clenched, he carefully opened the bedroom door, and to his dismay, saw Jessie and Sam in a compromising embrace.

They never saw Jim standing in the doorway. In a flash, Jim grabbed Sam by the hair and pulled him off Jessie, and she let out a scream. Sam hit the floor and Jessie saw the murderous glare in Jim's eyes. Jessie grabbed the blanket and pulled it up to her neck, and in horror watched as Jim kicked Sam in the groin. Sam doubled over with a groan, and as he lay on the floor paralyzed in pain, Jim turned to look at Jessie. She had never seen such rage in his eyes.

He grabbed Jessie's clothes off the floor and pulled her out of the bed. He shoved her in front of him down the hall and out the front door, throwing her clothes after her. From the back of the house Jessie heard the crash of glass breaking, and saw Sam limping for his horse. She just stood there in shock, wondering what Jim was going to do next. When he came to the back door, he looked hard into her eyes and said in a slow, deliberate tone, "I will be back in two hours. When I get back, I want you and your belongings out of this house and out of my sight."

Shaking with anger, he walked over to the buckboard, climbed in and cracked his whip over the horse. The horse lunged and the buckboard nearly tipped, then was hurdling down the dirt road leaving a cloud of dust behind. Jessie stood there for a moment, dazed, with no idea what to do next. Her life as a wife and mother had just been shattered in this most despicable folly. She knew in her heart that neither Jim nor

God Almighty would forgive such a disgraceful deed.

In his fury, Jim felt the urge to kill both Jessie and Sam. He had never felt so betrayed. It was a fortunate circumstance the three children were visiting their grandmother Mary for the week. When he returned home he carried two bottles of whiskey into the house and set about pouring them down his throat to salve his humiliation and rage.

A couple of days later, when he was supposed to pick the children up and bring them home, he went to Mary and told her what had happened. She wasn't too surprised, as she had suspected for some time that Jessie was having an affair. The whole town was whispering about it and she knew it was only a matter of time until Jim would find out. "Jim what do you plan to do," Mary asked.

"Mother, right now I

would love to kill them both,"
Jim said with tears in his
eyes.

"How many times in your
life can you be hurt badly
without wanting to retaliate?"
Mary asked as she put her
arms around Jim and let him
cry. He already had lost his
father, James in a shoot out,
now this time it looked like
he could also lose what he had
thought was the love of his
life.

After that Jim changed
dramatically. He seemed to be
angry at the whole world. Up
to that time there had never
been a divorce in the Quigley
family. His pride was
damaged beyond repair and he
ached with remorse for his
children. Mary had taken the
children into her home so they
would have the love and
family they needed at such a
difficult time. Jim went there
and spent as much time as
possible with them.

Chapter 24

Jim worked long hours trying to keep so busy he wouldn't think about the pain of the incident with Jessie and Sam. Mary tried to cheer him up, but the hurt was too deep. When he wasn't with his children he would go riding in the countryside or walking on the beach, searching for answers to ease his pain.

One day, about nine months after the incident, he was walking along the beach with his head down just watching the sand swirl in the ebbing waves. Jutting out from the shore was Battle Rock, a large formation that protruded out into the water at high tide. A lot of history is attached to that rock. Seventy-five years earlier there was a battle between the white seamen and the Indians. A great deal of blood was shed that week, until one man slipped down the ocean side of the rock and swam away for help. After that it was known as Battle Rock.

It was low tide and Jim had almost rounded the big rock when a young girl in her twenties was coming from the other side and almost bumped into him. "Oh! I'm so sorry! I didn't see you," he managed after the encounter.

"Yes," she laughed warmly, noticed!"

"Are you all right?" he asked, visibly shaking knowing his face was turning red, dropping his eyes and looking embarrassed

"Oh yes, I'm fine," she replied gazing into his eyes. "My name is Cora," she smiled. "and you are...?

"Jim, Jim Quigley," he smiled back. She was a lovely girl with blonde hair and sky-blue eyes. He couldn't stop looking at her. "Do you live near here? I haven't seen you before," he ventured.

"I've only been here about three weeks," she told him while making little circles in the sand with her bare toes. I'm living with my aunt just outside of Gold Beach. I like to come here and walk on the beach."

As they began walking along the sand together, she gazed out across the blue expanse and said, "The ocean makes me feel so small. It makes me wonder about where it ends and what it hides beneath its surface." She stopped then, and giving him a curious look said, "Well, I have to go now. Bye, Jim!" Then she was gone, running back the direction from which she had come.

Jim watched her disappear around Battle Rock, then stood there for a few minutes trying to sort out what had just happened. Was the girl real or just a figment of his overactive mind? He shook his head and began walking alone again, wondering about the encounter.

Time seemed to stand still for Jim. The following week he found himself in the judge's chambers, appearing for the final divorce decree from Jessie. It had been a year, yet Jim still felt a good deal of anger whenever he thought about how Jessie had betrayed him. He wondered if he would ever get over it. He was angry for himself, but deeply hurt for his children. Jessie rarely came to see them and Jim hoped he would never run into her when she did visit. There was no amnesty between them.

A couple of days after the divorce was final Jim was walking on the beach again. He saw the young blonde girl coming his way, so he waved. I guess she *was* real, he thought as she came closer.

"Hello, Jim," Cora said,

smiling. "It's nice to see you again."

"Hi, Cora," he smiled back. "It's nice seeing you, too. I hope I didn't appear to be rude when we met. I've just had a lot on my mind. I'd really like someone to talk to, if you don't have to run," he said raising his eyebrows in a questioning look.

"I guess I did sort of run away," she said avoiding his eyes. "I'm sorry. I just felt out of place, like you needed to be alone. But I would like to get acquainted, if you would," she spoke hesitatingly.

Jim nodded his head toward a flat rock a few feet away and they went and sat down. "I heard about your divorce from Jessie, Cora said softly."If you feel like talking, I'll just listen," she smiled.

Jim was surprised at how sweet and compassionate this

young woman was. His whole marriage to Jessie was constant upheaval after the second child had come. It seemed they had fought with nearly every word spoken, as Jessie grew more and more despondent. Now, sitting here beside him was someone who seemed to really care, someone who wanted to listen to him for a change. Maybe he had been wrong about his feeling towards women. Maybe they weren't all alike, after all. As they sat and talked that afternoon until the shadows grew long across the sand, Jim felt some of his anger drain away. Cora was a good listener and seemed to be a kind and gentle woman. She had made a lasting impression on Jim that day.

The summer faded into fall and Jim and Cora became close companions, spending a good deal of time riding through the forests or walking on the beach. She was fond of horses and had trained a few before moving to Gold Beach. She was a quick study for the breeding process and her gentility was an asset to green-breaking the colts and getting them ready for sale. She and Jim seemed to be made of much the same fabric and were becoming more and more woven together.

On Christmas Eve of 1926, Jim asked Cora to be his wife and she happily accepted. They had a small wedding with their closest friends and family in attendance. After building a new home in Port Orford, they enjoyed a long and happy marriage that lasted until Cora died in 1948. Noma and Bob build a small house across the highway from their home. Jim lived alone until his death in 1967.

Jessie had also remarried. She and Sam were wed shortly after her divorce from Jim. The marriage only lasted six months and Jessie was free once again.

Jessie then married Kelly
Welch a Montana ranch hand.
May 5 1956; he was killed in
a logging accident at a saw
mill in Port Orford Oregon.
The motor on the log bumper
had quit and when he tried to
repair it, the motor blew up
throwing Kelly into the water
dazed, he was trapped under
the logs, he drowned in three
feet of water. Jesse never
married again after that.

Noma and Stan spent the
summers with Jim and Cora
after their marriage, and Cora
got on well with them, but
they lived with Grandma Mary
Stone during the school year,
as it was more convenient for
them. James Evert had grown
into a fine young man and had
been talking about joining the
Army. In January of 1927 he
enlisted into the army as a
cook's helper. The world was
at peace as World War I had
ended and life was, for the
most part, getting back to
normal again.

A little more than a year

after his enlistment, while Evert was stationed in Denver, Colorado, a bunch of his buddies wanted to go to a movie one evening. It was a dull movie with no real plot, so he and his pals started fooling around and creating a ruckus. In the row in front of them were two young ladies getting obviously very upset with them. As one of them turned to say something to the rowdy bunch, Evert caught sight of lovely young lady sitting a couple of rows away. He crept over to the empty seat beside her and began quietly talking to her. From first glance she had stolen his heart away. His buddies saw his maneuver and began making remarks and loud kissing sounds, but he didn't hear them at all. At that moment all his attention was focused on the pretty young lady in the seat next to him, whose name was Loretta.

"Are you free tomorrow

night?" Evert asked with eyebrows raised in hope.

"Well-ll," Loretta hesitated, eyeing this handsome young man in uniform. "Yes," she finally told him, smiling coyly. "I do believe I am."

"Tell me where you live and I'll pick you up at seven tomorrow night," Evert whispered. That was the beginning of their whirlwind courtship, which resulted in marriage on the twentieth of April in 1928.

Pictures

Top right: James Evert and Loretta Myers wedding 1929

Top left:

Charlie Quigley with half

sisters Ruth and Bessie
Stone

Bottom:

Quigley kids left to right
Verla, Douglas, James
Stanley, Gertrude, Charline

Ruth, Charlie, Bessie 1905
Stone Quigley Stone

Everitt & Loretta Quigley 1929

L-R Verla, Douglas, Jim, Gertrude, Charline Quigley 1940

309

Chapter 25

Evert had told Loretta about Oregon and how beautiful it was there near the ocean, so when he was out of the Army they planned to move back there. He was sure his family would love her, and he hoped she would love living in Port Orford. In July of 1928, Evertt was honorably discharged from the Army. They packed their belongings, bid Loretta's family and friends farewell, and headed west to Oregon. Loretta had never seen forests so thick with trees and such beautiful ferns. She was overwhelmed by the immensity of the ocean and the long stretches of unspoiled beach. She had been raised in the city and, in her eyes; Oregon appeared to be almost untamed wilderness.

She didn't know quite what to think, as there were few stores for shopping and the selection of merchandise was quite limited. She found that most folks raised their own vegetables and fruit and did their own canning. One aspect of the country life that she found deplorable was the killing of farm animals for meat. She had never experienced such an act before, and Evert knew if she saw a cow or a chicken being killed she would most likely never eat meat again.

It was a new life and an exciting time for Loretta and Evertt. All his family was fond of Loretta and did what they could to help her adapt to life in Oregon. Evertt found a home outside of Port Orford where they set up housekeeping. A few months later, on the twenty-sixth of July in 1930, Loretta gave birth to a sweet baby girl weighing just five pounds, and named her Charline.

Nearly two years later, on the seventeenth of April in 1932, another baby girl was born and named Gertrude. Loretta had adapted to the manner of life in the country remarkably well, and kept an ample pantry of dried and canned goods from her garden. She was smart and clever and could improvise her way through most situations with true ingenuity.

Evert did the best he could to provide for his growing family, but often as not, the pay was meager and they had to be creative to make ends meet.

The following year, on the twenty-sixth of June in 1933, to their delight, a son was born and named James Stanley; in keeping with tradition (the first boy was always named James). A second boy, Douglas Harlow, was born on the sixteenth of September in 1935. Loretta and Evert had to work hard to keep their family clothed and fed, but with determination, they managed.

About that time Evert's brother, Stanley, relocated to Redmond, Oregon. He met and married a school teacher, Jean Riley, and they had one son, Clyde. Stanley bought a hardware store in Redmond and was quite successful considering the economy of the Depression.

After being in Oregon for seven years, Loretta was missing her family in Denver and wanted them to meet her children. She and Evertt talked about her going to Denver for a visit, and in June of 1936, her mother, Reta Myers, came to Oregon to help her make the trip back to Colorado with all the children. At the time Loretta didn't know that she was going to give birth again in February. Later she decided to remain in Denver for the birth of the fifth child, a girl, born on the seventeenth of that month in 1937.

Loretta named the

child Verna, and when she called Evertt on the phone to tell him about the new baby girl his response was cool. He said he didn't like the name and that he would never call her that. Loretta was confused about Evertt's attitude. She had never known him to behave that way, as he seemed to be pleased about the new baby girl. She thought perhaps he was upset that she had not talked to him first about a name for their little daughter.

One of her family suggested she change the "n" in Verna into an "L" and make the name Verla. So, hoping that would smooth Evert's feathers, she did just that. When Verla was only six weeks old Loretta, with all five children, boarded a bus back to Oregon. When she got home she noticed that Evert seemed to have changed somehow. She thought maybe it was because there were now five youngsters to feed and care for, placing a heavier burden on them both.

The atmosphere in their home was charged much of the time. Evert was gone every day until late at night after the children were all in bed. He and Loretta could be heard arguing from the children's rooms, and many nights Charline would cry herself to sleep. Gertrude was more outspoken and would show her anger and frustration, but often would take it out on the younger children. Loretta had her hands full and then some. With Evertt gone so much of the time it became a tremendous strain on her and she was often quite dejected.

Noma, Evert's sister, would come by now and then and offer to take one of the girls to their home for a weekend. She had married Bob Thompson, her grade school sweetheart, in Port Orford. In 1946, they built a lovely home

just off Highway 101. Bob
was well known as a
craftsman in the construction
business and did very well.
They had two daughters,
Joann and Adelle.

Verla was especially
fond of her Aunt Noma. She
loved visiting their home and
treasured the kindness and
warmth of their family. The
visits the girls made to their
Aunt's home helped them
through the despair they
endured at their own house.

Chapter 26

The Great Depression had taken a huge toll on most of the citizens of the United States and conditions continued to worsen. The Dust Bowl, which lasted for seven years, had struck the plains states of Oklahoma, Texas, Kansas, Colorado and Nebraska virtually destroying farm life there and causing inhabitants to seek other means of sustenance. Nearly eight hundred thousand people from the central part of the nation swarmed to California, the publicized land of opportunity, in hopes of finding employment and a better life.

In truth, most ended up picking crops for extremely low wages, and living conditions were generally less than acceptable. Migrant camps sprouted up like weeds, bread lines grew longer in the cities, and crime increased everywhere with the growing destitution.

War and unrest dominated the international political arena as Japan was expanding its empire while Germany and Italy were set to strike against the United States. As tensions grew during the second term of Franklin D. Roosevelt, unemployment soared. With the New Deal introduced during his first term, several programs were conceived and implemented by Congress in an effort to bring relief to a desperate population, some with impressive success. Even so, farmers had to be subsidized and jobs created to feed the nation's populace.

The Quigley's began moving from place to place as Evertt went from one job to another. Jobs were hard to come by, wages were meager and the hours long and arduous, placing immense strain on family.

One day in November of 1941, Evertt came home and told Loretta that he had taken a job on Wake Island, just north of Hawaii, as a cook for a large construction company.

He said he would only be there for about six weeks. The pay was very good, and it would give them the opportunity to get out of debt and get a larger house for the family. Evert suggested that during his absence Loretta's mother might come to Oregon to help her with the five children.

On the fifteenth of November in 1941, with much sadness and trepidation, the family waved good-bye to Evertt as he drove out of the driveway. An ominous cloud of dread pervaded their farewell.

Loretta's mother moved into the Quigley home in Roseburg, Oregon, where they had moved two years before Evert's departure to Wake

Island. She and Loretta carried on as best they could hoping Evert would return home at the end of the six weeks.

The political air was thick with discord and an ominous cloud of adversity hung over the entire nation. Japan had already invaded China and Indochina causing deteriorating diplomatic relations with the U.S. A special envoy from Japan met with Secretary of State Cordell Hull demanding that U.S. naval expansion in the Pacific be halted, and the release of frozen Japanese assets. On December sixth, President Roosevelt made a direct appeal to Japanese emperor, Hirohito.

On the seventh of December in 1941, there was a surprise attack by the Japanese, who flew over a peaceful, unsuspecting Pearl Harbor in Hawaii, dropping bombs on the U. S. Navy fleet anchored there. Chaos and terror reigned throughout the region as people ran in all directions screaming, no one knowing exactly what was happening. They were dying in the streets as squadrons of Japanese planes flew overhead releasing their lethal destruction on the island.

Sirens were blaring into the early morning as people scrambled for cover or to aid or rescue their friends. Ships in the harbor burned and smoke billowed in enormous clouds. The bombing continued relentlessly for hours, one strike after another by the Japanese warplanes. After what seemed like an eternity in hell, quiet skies finally prevailed over the smoking, ravaged city.

Nineteen ships, including five battleships and one hundred fifty planes had been destroyed, and more than two thousand three hundred military and civilians killed. On December eighth, Congress declared war against Japan.

Three days later Germany and Italy declared war against the United States.

In January of 1942, the United States received staggering industrial production goals from the President to support the war effort, and the armed forces were mobilized to deploy to Europe and Southeast Asia for combat. By great fortune, the U.S. aircraft carriers were not anchored in Hawaii at the time of the attack and so were able to swiftly play a major combat role in the Pacific against Japan.

On Wake Island, a few hundred miles from Hawaii, where Evert had gone, word came by short wave radio that the United States was at war with Japan. The inhabitants had no way to get off Wake Island, so they remained like sitting ducks waiting for any word or means of rescue to come. Help never did arrive, and on the twenty-fourth of

December the Japanese landed and came ashore taking everyone prisoner. The inhabitants, including Evert Quigley, were held at gunpoint on the beach for two days when, at last, a large ship appeared on the horizon flying a foreign flag.

There were about fifty men in all, forty Marines and about ten civilians. They were herded onto the ship like cattle and put in the hold where space allowed standing room only. The men were packed so tightly into the cramped space that Evert said a man died next to him and couldn't even fall down onto the floor.

After about a week at sea they sailed into the harbor at Hong Kong in a raging typhoon. The captives were blindfolded and taken to a filthy, stench-filled prison cell and were given nothing to eat but moldy bread and water rice with worms. The conditions were deplorable and the prisoners' physical and mental health was severely threatened as they faced a bleak future. Then they were lost to the war. Their families and friends could do no more than hope and pray for their return, if they thought they were even still alive.

Three years went by without any word from Evertt or his whereabouts. Not knowing whether he was alive or dead, Loretta moved back to Colorado to be closer to her family. Her Aunt Mae had some friends in Bremerton, Washington, who were encouraging her to go there and work in the shipbuilding yards. They said the money was good and they could provide a place for her to live.

Mae coerced Loretta to leave the children with their grandparents in Denver and travel to Washington with her to work. In need of an adequate income and not knowing Evert's status, Loretta finally agreed. They both took jobs as welders in the shipyards working varied shifts. The ladies who did that type of work were referred to as "Rosie the Riveter". Hundreds of women of all races achieved building over 747 ships during World War II.

One day in 1944, a friend called Loretta to tell her there were pictures and an article about the prisoners taken on Wake Island in the June issue of LIFE magazine, it showed photographs of some of the prisoners being held by the Japanese. Loretta rushed out to buy a copy, and with fear and anticipation she opened the magazine. About halfway through the pages of the article she let out a scream. "My God!" she shouted. "It's Evert!" He looked emaciated and had a beard and long hair, but she was certain it was her husband.

Amid tears of joy and hugs from her children and family, they read and re-read the article and stared disbelieving at the picture of Evert as a prisoner of the Japanese.

Picture from Life Magazine

Jap Photos of Interned American

GETTING THE NEWS—This picture, reproduced from the English-language propaganda magazine "Freedom" published by the Japs at Shanghai is to give their version of internment of U.S. subjects pending their exchange, purports to show a Lieutenant Malvada of Jap military press bureau notifying internees of British defeat at Singapore. Note Japs over-sized sword.

Daily Mountain News—Line Telephoto

DEVEREAUX OF THE MARINES propaganda magazine says this is a typical internment picture of Maj. James Devereaux, of Wake Island fame, quotes him, "After being south, it cold sprouting the winter here. Here we are supplied with every comfort."

On raised platform, Jap propaganda officer reads out to Shanghai military prisoners at Woosung. Japanese prisoners of Shanghai military area

of the U.S. Devereaux of the marines from Guam and Peking Wake Island district are present prisoners. There are also a few British officers held there under U.S. No...

Evertt Quigley   from Life Magazine   Sept 16,1942

Loretta, after numerous
attempts, and with the help of

friends, finally made contact with the Government about her discovery, seeking to verify if it really was Evert Quigley in the photograph. After several tense and disparaging weeks passed, Loretta received a reply from the Government advising her they had made contact with the Japanese embassy. The response was that it was, in fact, Evett Quigley in the magazine photograph and that he was indeed being held prisoner. In her excitement, Loretta wanted to talk to him right away, but being a prisoner of war, and with World War II still raging, she was instead given an address so she could write to him.

She judiciously wrote him numerous letters, never feeling certain that they would reach him, and praying that he would receive at least one. Newspapers printed heartbreaking stories of prisoners of war in Southeast Asia, and Loretta lived every day with intense fear in her heart. She prayed for the postman to deliver a letter, yet was afraid it would bring bad news. Her life had never hung in the balance as dramatically as during those weeks of waiting. Finally a postcard arrived addressed to Loretta, Charline and all the family. Loretta was relieved, but sad at the same time she knew he was still alive, but had no idea what shape he was in and any details she acquired were very scarce and indefinite.

A few months had passed when another postcard dated January 1, 1945, arrived from the Shanghai War-Prisoners' Camp, Barracks No.4-Sec't 2, addressed to Gertrude and Verla. It was a little late, but it was the best Christmas gift of all.

January 1, 1943

Dear Daughters & All,

Wrote to Charline last time, so will write to you this time. Hope you all had a nice Christmas and got a lot of presents. Wish you all a Happy New Year. How are you doing in school? Study hard and be good. Love to all from your Daddy.

Evert...
James E. Quigley

Due to prison restriction, only twenty-five words were permitted on the postcard. Evert could not disclose any information as to his location or his condition. He had been moved several times from one prison camp to another.

Loretta was relieved and grateful to know he was still alive and able to communicate, yet the foreboding in her heart still lingered. Weeks dragged into months of apprehension regarding the return of the prisoners and the waiting took a weary toll on her.

Five months after relocating in Bremerton, Loretta received letters from Charline and the older girls saying things were not going well at the grandparent's home and she needed to come home right away. It seemed as though the grandparents were not at all pleased with having Loretta's five children to care for and were apparently abusing her two sons, James Stanley and Douglas. Loretta boarded a bus and returned to Denver to take care of her children. Once again Loreta had a huge task before her; that of trying to raise the five children alone.

Chapter 27

History was made on the sixth of August in 1945, when the United States Air Force bomber, "Enola Gay", flew over the town of Hiroshima, Japan, and dropped an atomic bomb in an aggressive attempt to end the war. Again, on the ninth of August, another atomic bomb was dropped on the town of Nagasaki, killing and maiming thousands of people. The after-math of those bombings would continue to reap havoc for the people of Japan for decades to follow.

At last, on the second day of September in 1945, aboard the U.S.S. Missouri in Tokyo Bay, General Douglas MacArthur, Commander of the Southwest Pacific Fleet, along with Foreign Minister Mamoru Shigemitsu and General Yoshijiro Umezu signed the Japanese Surrender which ended World War II.

Evert was released soon after the end of the war and returned to the United States following five grueling years in Japanese prison camps. He was ill and had aged dramatically.

After he arrived in Denver in the fall of 1945, he tried to take a job, but could not mentally adjust to the responsibilities vital to caring for his family. His health had been severely compromised and he frequently suffered flashbacks and nightmares. A short time later, in a desperate effort to return to his home in Oregon, he loaded his family into a small car and made the trip to Port Orford, where he was welcomed with open arms by his family and friends.

Evertt struggled considerably after returning to Oregon. He just couldn't seem to get settled and his morale was dismally low. He found a small house in Port Orford for Loretta and the

five young children. To
Loretta's dismay Evert moved
himself into the house where
his mother, Jessie, lived. She
had married a man by the
name of Kelly Welsh from
Montana.

Kelly was years younger
than Jessie, but it was a good
marriage, and they seemed to
enjoy each other's company.
Jessie was more content with
her life in that marriage,
finally getting beyond her
former depression.

Evert and Kelly got on
well and Kelly was
understanding and
compassionate when Evert
would get moody and
irritable. There were no
programs in Port Orford to
help former prisoners re-enter
normal life after the
indescribable damage done in
the Japanese prison camps.
Actually few programs were
implemented anywhere, so the
former prisoners of war were
left to their own devices.
Severe cases were able to

enter a V.A. hospital for treatment, and that was oftentimes inadequate.

It was a tough time for Loretta, trying to raise the five children without their father at home. After enduring the hardships of Evert's absence and disappearance, she had suffered enormously. The disappointment of their marriage crumbling after all she had been through caused her much heartache and depression. Evert would come by the house occasionally, maybe once a week, to see that she had food. Eventually, Loretta could no longer endure the estrangement from her husband, so she came to a decision. She got together what money she could and filed for divorce.

Three years after Evert's return from the war, Evert and Loretta were divorced. In the spring of 1947, following the divorce, Charline and Gertrude were sent to Denver to live with their grandparents while Loretta settled affairs in Oregon. The next year she, Verla, James and Douglas also returned to live in the Denver area.

Not long after the divorce was final Evert married one of his former sweethearts, but that lasted only a few years. When that marriage grew sour, he withdrew and was once again troubled and alone.

Kelly and Evert built a small sawmill and tried going into business together making cedar shingles. Evert had bought twenty acres of old burned out timber north of the small town of Sixes, called Madden Butte in Curry county. A forest fire had burned most of the timber, leaving only tall snags standing. The Bandon Fire there had destroyed thousands of Fir, White Cedar and Myrtle Wood trees. Unfortunately the sawmill didn't go well due to Evert's failing health.

Kelly sold the small sawmill and took a job at a mill in Port Orford. On the morning of May 5, 1956, he failed to snap his safety belt on the log bumper, a small craft that was used to move logs from the millpond into the mill to be cut. Something went terribly wrong. He bent down to tend to a problem with the engine when there was a loud explosion, blowing Kelly off the craft. He landed unconscious and drowned in three feet of water before anyone could rescue him.

Once again Jessie found herself alone and grief-stricken over the loss of Kelly. Evert moved in with her so he could help her, but neither one of them was happy with that arrangement. They were both dealing with too much mental anguish and were moody and combative. They reached a point at which they could no longer tolerate each other's company, arguing almost constantly. Evert then moved away to a remote area east of Port Orford.

A few years later Jessie was put in a nursing home after suffering a stroke. Not long afterward, Evert also went into a nursing home in Bandon, Oregon, where he died on the second of January in 1973, from a heart attack. Jessie was never told about Evert's death.

While in the nursing home, Jessie discovered that Lois was in the same facility. She remembered how, many years earlier, Lois had made a play for Jim when he and Jessie were sweethearts. She became very upset and said she was going to get even with her. She was on her way to Lois's room at a determined pace when the nurses caught sight of her and ran to intervene. Jessie screamed, "Just let me at her! She's gonna pay for what she done to me!"

The nurses managed to

restrain Jessie, and moved Lois to another part of the nursing home. Later, it had become the saga of the nursing home, and brought forth occasional chuckles from the nurses. That feisty old gal, Jessie, finally passed away on the twenty-fifth of January in 1977, at the incredible age of ninety-eight.

Chapter 28

While Evert was a prisoner of war, his Grandmother Mary, and her husband, John had moved to Portland Oregon, where they lived out the remainder of their lives. Evert went there to visit them a few times after he returned to the States. Seeing how Evert suffered with all the problems related to being imprisoned in Japan and his divorce from Loretta, as well as her own loss of James, it would suffice to say that Mary had lived through more heartbreak than most women today could endure.

Mary Louise came to visit her mother once each year bringing her lavish gifts from her travels. After several years of performing in theaters she left New York and took up residence in England. She continued to perform there and loved it so that she remained, married, and had a family. Some said she even performed for the Royal Family on occasion. At least she had some wonderful stories to tell her grandchildren about her travels and performances.

Loretta was informed by Gertrude that she was going to marry John Holcomb, whom she had been dating for about six months. Gertrude was a junior in high school and Loretta did not agree to the marriage. John was 21 and working at a hardware supply where he had been employed for a year. After numerous arguments and discussions, Loretta finally gave in to simply put an end to the turmoil. In 1949, Gertrude and John were wed and a baby came to them before the year's end. Their son was named Jerry David, and John was very proud to be a father.

Charline, at age eighteen, married Charles Anthony, and they had a daughter Verla Lorraine the following year. She and Gertrude seemed to be in competition, as that same year not long after their marriages, the girls ended up moving back to Oregon where they both met and fell in love with the same man, Charles Nichols. They each divorced their husbands after very brief marriages and then Gertrude became pregnant by Charles. He refused to marry her saying he was in love with Charline. In an effort to put that life behind her, Charline left Oregon and returned once more to Denver. Eventually she remarried and had three daughters and one son with her second husband, Bud Lewis.   For the better part of her marriage to Bud, Charline and her family lived in Washington. Charline divorced Bud and moved not far from Mount St. Helens, a volcano that erupted violently on the eighteenth of May in 1980. The debris avalanche and blowing ash that occurred after the eruption affected the entire area for miles surrounding the volcano. The Toutle River valley was filled with rock, silt, and ash causing the river to rise considerably above its normal capacity.

Charline were forced to leave her home because the area water sources became polluted due to the ash and dramatic geological changes resulting from the eruption. To prevent flooding, the Toutle and Cowlitz Rivers had to be dredged to move the debris and silt downstream. Everything within one hundred fifty miles was covered with deposits of ash from the blast.

A few years later Charline was diagnosed with kidney problems, which developed into cancer and took her life. Speculation was that all the pollution from the volcanic eruption caused the cancer, as there were a number of cases diagnosed as kidney cancer from the area surrounding Mount St. Helens.

Gertrude gave birth to a daughter, Stacy, by the liaison with Charles, and shortly afterward went back to her husband, John, for a brief period of time. He left her after a year, found a new love and remarried. A couple of years later Gertrude met and married Chuck Matthews. He was a kind and caring man who had no children from his previous marriage. He was very fond of Gertrude's daughter, Stacy, and was exceptionally good to her.

Tragically, Stacy developed a brain clot and died at the tender age of thirteen. Gertrude took her daughter's death extremely hard and suffered chronic depression. Just two years after Charline's death, at age fifty-nine, Gertrude had a massive heart attack which ended her turbulent life.

Douglas married a

couple of times after his tour of duty in the Korean War. He stayed in the Denver area and had three children, then eventually divorced he mains single today.

James Stanley married several times fathering four children. He ultimately ended up single and remained in Colorado in the Denver area.

Verla married Richard Clemens April 5 1953 had two sons Marvin Kim he married Karen Kraft they had two children Nick Carter and Shannon Lee. Roger H. Clemens married Irene Rivera they had 2 sons Jordan and Zack. Daughter Sandra Lugene married Ernie Myers; they had three children Koreen Leann, Daniel Lee, and Brian. Richard and Verla were divorced, but were remarried ten years later June 27 1989. She gave birth to a third son who she named James Clinton, in keeping with the James name that had been in the family history for so many years.

Fourteen years later they were divorced again. Verla left Colorado and returned to Oregon for a few years to open a business in the small town of Beaver Oregon on the coast. She then moved to San Diego and on to Arizona. In her retirement she pursues a number of interests, including writing and photography.

Loretta had returned to Oregon with her daughter, Gertrude, and remained there after Gertrude's death. She never remarried as she had suffered greatly and never felt secure in trusting men again after Evert left her. A short time after Gertrude die she moved to Forest Grove, Oregon, to reside in a nursing home until her death on the eighth of April in 1995.

EPILOGUE

Justin Turner leaned back against the car while Louise and I stood there holding our breath. "Well," he said, "if you look about a thousand feet up on that hill over yonder, that's where your Great-grandfather is buried."

I couldn't believe it! We'd done it! We had finally found his grave after one hundred sixteen years. It was like finding the pot of gold at the end of the rainbow.

I could hardly wait to get back in the car and drive up to see it. I drove up as close as I could to the grave, parked and ran the rest of the way. It was about fifty feet off a rutted pasture lane. There I was, standing by his grave on the hill where all I could hear was the wind blowing, and strange as it may seem, I swear I could hear cheers and laughter from somewhere beyond.

It was as if my Great-grandfather, James Quigley, and all those related to him that had passed on, were rejoicing with me. At last, someone had made the effort to find out where his bones were laid to rest.

It was a bittersweet moment, seeing as it had taken this long for someone in the family to find his grave. All the stories I had heard as a child proved to be untrue. He hadn't been buried under the trees, as the nearest tree was at least a thousand feet away and all around was nothing but desert. At Cow Springs there were old cottonwood trees and an old house, but nothing more. As I stood there with all the mixed emotions of joy and sorrow, I could close my eyes and picture the shooting taking place, the pain, heartbreak, and then quiet for one hundred sixteen years.

I couldn't wait to get back home in Arizona and call my ninety-four-year-old Uncle Stanley, who lives in Langlois, Oregon, and is a grandson of James. He was thrilled and wanted to know if I had taken pictures and, of course, I had.

Uncle Stan was happy to finally learn the truth about where his Grandfather was buried. He said his Grandmother, Mary Stone, didn't talk much about the shooting, and she never spoke an unkind word about James.

In October of 2002, while traveling in the Four Corners area with my friend, Sandra, I came across some cast iron horse heads at a place in Mancos, Colorado, and on impulse bought them, having no idea what I was going to do with them.

One night about a week after returning from Cow

Springs, I awoke in the middle of the night like I'd been struck. I knew what I was going to do. I could make a nice marker for James' grave using those horse heads; perhaps this was a way to honor Great-grandfather James. It's the least I can do for him. After all, if it weren't for him I wouldn't even be here.

From that time on it was like he was right there with me, encouraging me in many ways. Strange as it may sound, when I began writing the GRAVE QUEST it was as if James was looking over my shoulder the whole time telling me the story to write.

I called my brother, Douglas Quigley, who lived in a small town just outside of Denver, and told him about finding the grave. He, too, was elated to know I had accomplished my quest. His wife, Nancy agreed to come down for a visit and help with putting the marker on the grave.

I went to a rock shop where I got a piece of marble and had his name, date of birth, and date of the shooting by John Dodson engraved on it. About a month later I sent a letter to Justin asking him if it would be all right to come over and clean up the grave and put the marker on it. He replied that it would be fine, so when Douglas arrived I had everything ready to take to Cow Springs.

I had a brainstorm just before Douglas arrived. Since the horse heads were hollow, perhaps I could put together a time capsule of sorts, adding a little mystery to the setting. I then proceeded to put together the story of James, pictures of his three sons, and a family history up to the present day.

Included with some other memorabilia was some information from the current time describing the sad story of 9-11-01, when terrorists struck the World Trade Center in New York. Who knows? Maybe in another hundred years someone else will go looking for James' grave and solve the mystery of **TCIHH**, which is written on his headstone. It stands for "Time Capsule In Horse Head."

I wish to express my gratitude to Justin Turner and his family for keeping the grave intact for all those years, and all those who lived there before the Turners, as well.

To you, Great-grandfather James Quigley, thank you for a wonderful and fulfilling journey back into a time gone by from your Great-granddaughter, Verla (Quigley) Clemens, in the year of our Lord, 2003. I hope this book meets with your approval.

MAY YOU

REST IN PEACE

James Quigley
10-15-1859 = 6-29-1886

Acknowledgments

I would like to acknowledge the following people for their contributions and support in making this book possible. To my Uncle Stanley Quigley the only living grandson of James Quigley for his extraordinary memory of the Quigley family history. To Kelly West, Clyde Quigley, Douglas Quigley for their information resources and support. Louise Johnson, for her encouragement, willingness to be adventurous and read all those microfilms.

Much gratitude to all those kind folks at the Silver City Museum, Public Library of Microfilms, Silver City Enterprise Newspaper, WMMU Miller Library, and the Church of Jesus Christ of Latter Day Saints, who assisted in searching old records and microfilms in Silver City, New Mexico.

A special thanks to the Justin Turner family of Cow Springs, New Mexico, for their kindness and cooperation in the final steps of my GRAVE QUEST.

Verla Quigley Clemens

BIB
LIO
GR
AP
HY

THE MARY D HUME

The Last Steam Powered
Artic Whaler

By Betty Van Leer and
Captain Ed Shields

1984 Curry County Historical
Society

920 South Ellensburg

Gold Beach Oregon 97444

Church of Jesus Christ
of Latter Day Saints

(Family History)

3755 North Swan

Silver City, New Mexico

505-538-3844

Silver City Museum

312WestBroadway

Silver City, New Mexico
88061

Research Library

Extensive Index of Local
Newspapers

Public Library of
Microfilms

515 W College Ave

Silver City NM 88061

505-538-3672

Silver
City
Enterpri
se
Newspa
per
WMMU
Miller
Library
July 30,
1886

World War II Bombing
of Pearl Harbor and Taking

of Wake Island.

News articles from scrap book of Loretta Quigley

    The Butterfield Overland Mail - Stitching the Country together.